After paying off their first h[...]
having bought and paid o[...]
properties in the following [...]
release equity in one to bu[...]
lives in the Brisbane Valley, Queensland, with her
husband, Jim, their two young sons and their menagerie
in the family's new dream home. Anita is an energetic
full-time mother and independent businesswoman (Jim
notes that she has one overworked employee: him). She
relaxes by painting, fishing, riding her horses and writing
thrillers for the whole family.

www.anitabell.com

NOTE: If purchasing an investment property in Australia,
be sure to read the Australian version of this book FIRST
as there are a great many differences to be wary of.

YOUR INVESTMENT PROPERTY

HOW TO CHOOSE IT, PAY FOR IT AND TRIPLE YOUR RETURNS IN 3 YEARS

BY SOMEONE WHO DID IT IN 2

ANITA BELL

RANDOM HOUSE
NEW ZEALAND

National Library of New Zealand Cataloguing-in-Publication Data

Bell, Anita, 1967– .
   Your investment property: how to choose it, pay for it and
   triple your returns in 3 years / Anita Bell.

   ISBN 1 86941-545-0

   1. Real estate investment. 2. Real estate business. I. Title.

332.6324–dc 21

A RANDOM HOUSE BOOK
published by
Random House New Zealand
18 Poland Road, Glenfield, Auckland, New Zealand
www.randomhouse.co.nz

This edition first published 2002, reprinted 2003 (twice), 2004

ISBN: 1-86941-545-0

Typeset by Midland Typesetters, Victoria, Australia
Printed and bound by Griffin Press

Contents

Acknowledgements

This book is dedicated to those thousands of readers
who stopped me in the street to thank me for the first
one and ask for more, and to my wonderful family who
supported me in the process.

And also to
Pam Chamberlain and Cheryll Levick
who taught me that fair and decent real estate agents
do exist.

Introduction

Welcome to the wonderful world of investment loans and property. With this book I hope to answer all of your questions and more about buying and selling properties for profit. But you can also use or adapt many of the tips and shortcuts in here to buy or sell holiday homes, business premises, hobby farms or live-in fixer-uppers.

For those who don't know me from my first books, I must warn you that I have absolutely no formal qualifications whatsoever in the real estate or banking industries. Everything you're about to read is from personal experience gathered while I bought and paid off my own home PLUS three investment properties between the ages of sixteen and twenty-six. (And all of them in less than three years each while earning only low to middle incomes and without having to borrow against one to buy another.) There are also shortcuts and traps I discovered from helping to rescue others—free of charge of course, because unlike many other finance authors, I'm not involved in the finance industry.

Your Mortgage **is for people starting out with a clean slate.**
Your Money **is to help you get and keep a clean slate.**
Your Investment Property **is for people with or without a clean slate.**

My immediate goal is to keep your initial costs down, by focusing each book on self-contained specific financial goals, depending on your needs at any one stage in life. That's why the chapter on selling your home quickly is in this book, not in *Your Mortgage.*

One last note before we begin
My goal of buying and paying out investments as fast as possible so I can move on to the next one debt-free is definitely NOT what you'll hear from any other investment specialist that I'm aware of. Even the reputable advisors seem to focus on debt maximisation and tax minimisation, aiming for capital gain in the long term, while I focus on minimising costs and maximising profits in the short term, using tax minimisation as an accelerator with capital gain as a bonus.

Why such different approaches? Well, I think of it as just two ends of the same solution, and the multitude of packages that get offered to you in the investment marketplace usually fall towards the far end from how I prefer to invest in property. My choice is based on the fact that I like to live debt-free and I've learned how to get the best out of every cent that passes through my pocket in order to do that.

The debt maximisation argument is based on the assumption that you don't mind being in debt and that you already are doing the best you can with your personal finances. We can debate the pros and cons of each side until we're all blue in the face, because neither side is right or wrong. However, knowing that my alternative exists should arm you with the knowledge and confidence you need to find your own happy medium for your own circumstances. And yes, many of the tips and hints in this book should still apply to all reputable investment programs even if they involve big debt.

Sadly, no-one teaches us about money management

early on, so a lot of sensible, hardworking people are falling behind despite their best intentions. Too often, they're sinking way over their heads in debt and paying twice what they need to, while they're chasing 'future projections of growth', instead of minimising debt and maximising profits to get ahead of the pack in leaps and bounds in the short term. But more on that later. Just remember that no matter what path you choose for investment, always do what FEELS right for YOU. Money is only part of the equation for financial success. Fun and contentment should play a big part too.

> Don't commit to any investment program you don't like the sound of or can't completely understand. Because when it comes down to it, it's personal preference, basic maths and common sense that still reign supreme.

Now let's get cracking, shall we? Grab yourself a pack of colourful highlighters, because I'm just busting to share some of my favourite investment property fun . . .

ANITA BELL'S FORMULA
FOR INVESTMENT PROPERTY SUCCESS

Get the best out of investments in the short term by lowering your costs. (The biggest cost is interest so pay things off quickly.)

Then increase the property's ability to earn income while minimising tax where possible and aim to succeed on that.

Capital gain can then be your bonus, not something you rely on to survive or progress.

Then aim to keep or invest your returns from three sources (property income, tax refunds and capital growth on a debt-free property) instead of pumping your profits and equity for the next 20 years into your bank's already big coffers.

1

Are You Ready to Buy, or Are You Just a Sitting Duck?

YOUR FIRST CHOICE: A PROPERTY FOR YOU OR A PROPERTY FOR YOUR WALLET?

If you've never owned property before, you might be wondering if the first property you buy should be your own home or an investment property—perhaps to help fund the purchase of your own home later on. Many first-time property buyers get incredibly uptight trying to forecast which will be best for them financially. But the long-term financial outcome is only a small part of your decision. You'll want to take convenience and lifestyle into consideration too. So while your decision may seem complicated, there's really no need to break into a fretful sweat about it. Simply consider the following five main points.

1. **You can't use interest as a tax deduction on a property if you've already lived in the property yourself.** (Unless you're positive gearing. See definition on page 22. But don't let a lack of tax benefits stop you from renting while you're away on a long holiday if you would appreciate the extra cash, not to mention live-in housesitters to help keep the burglers at bay while you're away.)

2. **Only a portion of your expenses will be tax deductible if a portion of the property is used for private purposes.** (If you live in part of it, for example.) NOTE: Different rules can be applied in numerous ways to decide the tax deductible percentage allowable, depending on what type of investment property it is, whose names it was purchased in, what expenses are being claimed and what contractual arrangements you can make for the sublease or rental of the place, so see your accountant for details of your options for your specific situation.

3. **Not everyone has a personality or lifestyle that suits buying your own home.** There's nothing wrong with that, so don't feel pressured in any way to conform. Instead, consider this simple table of situations:

If you've ticked off boxes in both columns then there's still no reason to fret yet. Simply read on to see if investment in property suits your goals, lifestyle and personality *after* you learn what you're getting yourself in for . . .

The next thing you need to do if you're thinking about investing in property, is figure out if you're ready to be a property manager—emotionally as well as financially. And yes, that's even if you intend to pay an agent to handle most of the day-to-day management of your portfolio. You need to figure out if you'll be able to sleep at night when

You'll usually feel happier buying your own home first and an investment property later on, if one or more of the following applies to you	You'll often be happier financially and socially buying an investment property ahead of your own home if one or more of these points applies to you
If you're sick of the rent cycle—or of living with your parents.	If you're single and don't like the idea of mowing the lawn or keeping up with all the bills and home maintenance by yourself.

If you can handle the idea of living in one place for a few years.	If your employer or family provides you with cheap housing, so you don't really need to pay for the roof over your head yet.
If you would enjoy the security of owning your own home.	If you're likely to be transferred regularly or at least once within the next three years. (Hands up everyone who hates packing boxes!)
If you'd like to keep pets that your landlord won't allow.	If you would need extra income from the property to help make repayments or can't afford repayments on a mortgage unless the property makes an income to help you support it. (Warning: You must have a back-up plan to make repayments out of your own pocket whenever the property is vacant, or you run a higher risk of losing everything.)
If you don't need income from the property to help make repayments (eg. rent from tenants).	If you have a business which could be more profitable if you get loan repayments for its premises to be less than what you'd have to pay in leases.
If someone in your family has special health or hobby needs that only a purpose-built building can provide. For example, timber floors for children who suffer allergies, or ramp access for aged or disabled people, or a darkroom for photography enthusiasts etc.	If you parents, uncles or other relatives want to leave property to you in their will and if they prefer to transfer it to you while they're still alive instead of risking it falling subject to litigation and death taxes after they've kicked the bucket.
	If you have an opportunity to purchase a bargain in an area that's unsuitable for your own use (but which you can easily afford).
	If you pay a lot of tax and would like a lot of it back to roll into your investments and make them grown faster. (Although any reputable investment that's geared in ways to keep the Inland Revenue Department (IRD) happy will get you that.)

your tenants are throwing wild parties or breeding free-range budgerigars in the living-room of what amounts to be your life savings. And you need to know of the potential rip-offs at every stage along the purchase-to-sale path.

HOW TO TELL IF YOU'RE READY, AND WHY THAT MAKES YOU VULNERABLE

Use the following table to help you find out if you're suffering any of the symptoms of being financially and psychologically ready to invest in property, while at the same time, seeing why each point makes you vulnerable.

You're ready to invest in property if you suffer ALL of the following symptoms	But you're vulnerable at this stage because
a) You're earning an income that has tax sucked out of it in whopping chunks every pay, and feel a desperate urge to invent a new swear word when you add up what you and your partner have paid in tax over the last five years.	Investment foxes can lure you with promises of getting back all your tax every pay, easily and legally by using investment schemes set up in a similar way to the reputable programs. At the same time, they keep your attention off their very nasty fine print, not to mention the fat income they're syphoning from your wallet behind your back. And even some reputable schemes can slug you with extortionate management fees.
b) You develop an unconquerable urge to read everything you can about investing in property; if you can't help but walk slowly past a real estate agent's display window; and if you find yourself dwelling on the real estate pages of your newspaper, when you used to just skip to the TV guide or cartoons.	Investment foxes can convince you that investing in property is complicated and confusing. They'll suggest the choice is too wide for one person to keep up with when you're not involved in the industry every day, and they'll say their advice will simplify things for you and get you the best deal possible in the marketplace at the time.

	There's nothing wrong with employing a property manager, however, so finding the line between reputable and rip-off can be very tricky if you're not on the lookout.
c) You own your own home, or you're coping nicely with repayments and still have money spare in your monthly budget to top up repayments on another property. (You'll have rental income from the second property and you can apply for tax breaks to put towards repayments too. So the top-up amount from your own pocket may be as little as twenty bucks a fortnight, depending on the mortgage and rental income etc.)	Investment foxes—especially those in cahoots with developers and lenders—see dollar signs in front of their eyes and drool at the opportunity to sucker all that equity and potential equity back out of your pocket. They'll try to convince you that property debt is good debt—which it is, but only to a point. They'll explain quite reasonably how releasing equity from your home to buy others will help you build a bigger portfolio faster—which it will, but at a price. You can say goodbye to debt-freedom in your working lifetime. What makes the difference between reputable and rogue advisors here is that reputable advisors clearly explain the risks and their expenses, while the rogues will divert your attention from the kickbacks they're getting by herding you to the investments that benefit their pocket the most.
d) You've got a wretched feeling in your gut that other people are getting financially ahead, further and faster than you.	Investment foxes will lure you with schemes which promise shortcuts to phenomenal wealth, while they work out of their mum's garage and owe 80% or more on that red Porsche they drive, trying to impress you.

SITTING DUCK DETECTOR

Now that you know where your vulnerabilities lie, let's try this quick quiz to see if you have the absolute basic knowledge or instincts to keep you safe from the sly foxes of the property investment world—or if you're just a sitting duck for them. I've included questions here for each stage of buying, owning and selling an income-producing property, but these are only a small sample of the skills you need, so if you ace the test, don't get too excited yet. Even more importantly, don't fret if you fail at this early stage either. That's what this book is for—to help you learn how to make better choices.

When shopping for an investment

1. *Would you use a 'Rule of 72' in order to:*
   a) know when you've looked at enough properties before deciding which one to buy?
   b) know when you've asked enough questions about the place before signing a contract?
   c) roughly work out in your head, how long it will take for your new debt and/or your new property values to double?

2. *When a real estate agent says 'Let's go check out that property' do you:*
   a) get in their car with your parents, partner or friend in the back seat?
   b) take your car, with the agent riding in the passenger seat giving directions?
   c) drive your car, following theirs?

3. *If a real estate agent lets it slip that there are other people looking at the same property do you:*
   a) frown, feeling pressure to rush your decision?
   b) nod, weighing things up in your head quickly to make an offer before anyone else gets a chance?
   c) smile, confident that bargains are everywhere and that of course other people would be interested in it, otherwise it wouldn't be worth much as an investment property?

When shopping for the loan

4. *To select your lender, do you:*
   a) go through the lender recommended to you by the property developer or investment advisor who organised the purchase for you?
   b) go to the bank that handles all your other savings accounts, credit cards and other loans?
   c) investigate a handful of lenders, including your own bank and an assortment of others that have been around for a long time, just to see if you're still getting close to the best deal?

5. *After having an investment loan rejected by the lender of your choice, would you:*
   a) go back to the developer/investment advisor and ask if they can help you get finance?
   b) keep approaching different lenders until you find one that will approve your loan?
   c) ask why you've been rejected and do whatever it takes to get accepted somewhere next time?

6. *When selecting your loan, what is most important to you:*
   a) lowest possible repayments per month?
   b) lowest possible deposit?
   c) lowest possible interest rate?

When signing contracts

7. *Your real estate agent will set a settlement date for the purchase, which is usually somewhere between four and six weeks from the date you sign the contract. Do you:*
   a) ask for a shorter settlement date—like within a week or fortnight so you can get into the place and start making money?
   b) accept whatever settlement period you're offered, and try to organise yourself around that?
   c) ask for a longer settlement period—perhaps six to twelve weeks—with access to the place as soon as finance is approved, so you can sneak some

payments off your principle, organise tenants and refurbish so you can earn higher rent from day one, without any repayments to make in the meantime?
8. *When your bank manager asks you for a date that's convenient to get a valuation on your other properties, do you:*
   a) open your diary and organise a date?
   b) ask why a valuation on your other properties is needed?
   c) tell them you don't need or want valuations on any other properties, because you're buying this property at a bargain price but with a 20% (or more) deposit on its *true* value, so the valuation of it by itself will be more than enough security for the loan you're asking for.

> See Appendix I for quiz scoring of my sitting duck detector.

HOW TO PROTECT YOURSELF
- finish reading this book
- ask questions of your real estate, loan or investment advisors at every stage
- be suspicious, be verrry suspicious

Doing these three things will transfer the power into YOUR hands, where it belongs. You shouldn't feel like a pup on a leash when you choose a property or sign contracts. You should be the one that's in control!

Yes, it's wise to ask for advice, but it's even wiser to ask that advice from two or three different sources, compare their answers and test them against your own gut instinct. Hopefully, this book will arm you with all the major questions you need to ask. But *never underestimate your own good judgment* and common sense.

THREE GOLDEN RULES FOR INVESTMENT

1. *Listen to your inner voice,* because if any aspect of an investment sounds peculiar, it either IS peculiar or you haven't asked enough questions about it yet to understand it properly.
2. *Never enter into ANY contract or investment unless it FEELS right for YOU.* No investment is worth losing sleep over—no matter how good the promised returns will be.
3. *Never pay more than you have to.*

TRANSFER THE POWER INTO YOUR HANDS

Treat each meeting with real estate agents, investment advisors and money lenders as if you're an employer looking for new staff—which you basically are. You're going to pay these people, either directly or through the vendor, to provide you with a service, so you have a right to the best service possible.

Try asking them: Why you should go with them, instead of any of their competitors. How long have they worked in the industry? What was the last industry seminar they attended, and when? What does their personal property portfolio consist of? Do they have brochures about their agency and sample contracts that you can take away to read? Ask them to declare in every way the extent to which they will profit from your involvement in their scheme/purchase or development. (eg. Do they get spotters' fees, commissions or bonuses of any kind paid to them by the lenders or developers who are also involved? Basically, you want to know: 'What's in it for

---

Never be afraid to ask questions.
Advisors are paid to advise, so help them do
their job by asking lots of them.

you, aside from your standard commission? And how much is that, all up?')

Then for real estate agents in particular, ask to see their current proof of membership to the Real Estate Institute (REINZ). NOTE: I've put a blank table in Appendix III to help you record and compare answers.

Then, before agreeing to accept their services—and certainly before signing anything—go home and think about every word you've been told. Now that you're alone and there's no pressure on you, jot down every question that pops into your head even if you need more than a full page for them. Then call your advisor or real estate agent and ask them each of your questions, noting answers on that page and ticking them off as you go. Circle any that they need to double check and get back to you about— and make sure you don't sign anything until they do. And remember to approach two or three agencies, and compare results to make your choice easier.

FOR THE PROCRASTINATORS

You may still be confused about whether property—ANY property—is really the right investment vehicle for you. There are so many choices these days that your brain may threaten to explode if your fingers so much as caress the folds of another investment brochure. There's shares, bonds, debentures, managed funds and superannuation to choose from—and that's just a fraction of the main categories. They all have multitudes of subcategories with all kinds of choices and options. But they're all forecast heavily on aspects that are beyond the control of any one person or company. So it's highly possible that you may reach a stage where you just want to give up looking for a while.

Please don't.

Your choices are certainly wide, but there's no real reason to give yourself heartburn considering them. Bring yourself some comfort instead by reading on to the next section.

PROPERTY VERSUS STOCKMARKET—MY RUN-IN WITH THE AGE-OLD DISPUTE

For years, I listened to stockbrokers telling me how fabulous investment in shares can be, while real estate agents filled my head with promises of great returns, and investment advisors told me I should diversify into both. But as an L-plate investor who understood how much extra you pay for items when you pay them out over the longest time, I knew I couldn't afford both.

I had to choose.

So I sat down in the paddock one day with my horse and listed the pros and cons of each on a long sheet of foolscap (which Apache kept trying to eat). And I'm ashamed to say that even where the list made my choice obvious—mathematically as well as logically—fear still ruled my final choice.

Do I regret my choice for one second? Definitely not.

Yes, I could see that shares were better for me in both the long and the short terms. But property *felt* better. I was twenty-three and debt-free. I knew loans and how to get them working for me, so I stayed within my comfort zone. I swayed to my family's advice that placing bets at the TAB and buying shares on the stockmarket had about the same chance of success, and so continued to steer clear of the stockmarket. Better the devil you know, hey?

Instead, I bought and paid out my investment property in only twenty-two months. Then I found that I was faced with exactly the same choice again—shares or property. Only this time I wanted more of a challenge, so I decided it was time to take the plunge. (Since that day, my average return from the sharemarket has been 12% to 70% tax clear a year—and it's only low when I spend most of my time writing because I prefer the stress-free, lower risk purchases that don't chain me to the stock reports.)

But still, having stuck my toes into both investment pies with reasonable success, I hope this quick comparison of the main points that affected me will help you too. (Remember, it's the option you feel most comfortable with that you should ultimately choose. Then stretch your toes into the other pie only when—or if—you're ready.)

Investing in property	Investing in shares of companies listed on the stock exchange
ON THE PLUS SIDE • Land is a finite resource. They're not making any more— canal estates excluded—so most land MUST gain in value over the long term as the population increases. • Someone somewhere will always see value in land, but a company is only as good as its employees, management, distribution, advertising and product. • It feels good to own property. • You can drive past a property to check how it's going, but you only have financial reports to check on the progress of your companies. • You can diversify in property by diversifying the types of properties you own—eg. houses, industrial sheds, shops or units—as well as which suburb, city or province you buy them in. ON THE MINUS SIDE • You can't sell off a bathroom if you need ten grand in three days' time. • Tenants can be a pain in the back pocket—and other places too. • Agent's commission can be higher too. • Sales take months to finalise.	ON THE PLUS SIDE • Shares cost less to get in and out of. • Shares don't lock up giant sums of money into one place. • Income stream from shares with-dividends is better than from property. • Dividends can have 'imputation credits' which means that tax has been paid for them*, but you have to pay tax on any income you get from property. • Over the last 15 years, industrial shares have risen an average of 15% compound, compared with only 8% for house prices in main cities. ** • There are no legal fees involved. • No vacancies, repairs, thieves, tenants or acts of God to worry about. • Sales take only three days to finalise. ON THE MINUS SIDE • When you buy, you have to get cash to your broker in three days. (Not so bad if your bank has electronic banking facilities.) • Big investors and financial commentators often spook the market with words like 'crash' or 'slump' when often only a few bigger companies are going through a price correction.

NOTES

* *Imputation credits* means the dividends are fully franked—two technical-sounding terms which just mean that the company has paid the full rate of company tax on the profits it makes, so you only have to make up the difference between the company tax rate and yours. But since the company tax rate is 30% (effective 1 July 2001 but tax-paid basis effective from 1 July 2002) many middle income earners—and all low income earners—will actually get tax back on any fully franked income from shares. On the other hand, you have to pay the tax on income from property investment unless you've got whopping debts over it, so your expenses cancel out your income. And where's the profit or fun in that?

** Speaking technically for a tick, these figures suggest a geared share portfolio would return more than 28% a year, while the property portfolio equivalent might return only 16%. But still, 16% is better than what you're getting at the moment by not investing at all, so don't be afraid to go for it, using the property checklists in this book to make sure you really max out your potential for gain.

> Of course, shares and property don't rise
> at the same rate or time.
>
> Usually, property values fall, not long before
> share prices start to rise
> and vice versa.

WARNING: IF YOU LOSE YOUR JOB

Income from rental properties is considered normal income for the dole and other income-tested benefits. So if you lose your job, you're expected to cop a reduction or loss of benefits—regardless of whether or not your rental income is going straight into repayments on the property. Decidedly unfair I think, considering that we're all supposed to be funding our own retirements as best we can and that some people have chosen investment property as a vehicle for doing that. (In a sense, the investment properties are all that many people have for super-annuation—and nobody else is expected to suck dry their superannuation fund before they're entitled to unemployment benefits. But what can you do, when the government makes the rules?)

So plan for losing your job. Slog a few thousand in extra repayments off your investment property so that if the worst happens, you have a safety net to withdraw from and live off until you find another job. (NOTE: Mortgage protection insurance will make your repayments for you at the minimum monthly rate, but they usually won't start until all your extra repayments have been used up first— another nasty trap that you need to be aware of.)

Never fund all of your investments through the one lender at the one time—whether that's for shares or property or any combination of the two—because you're leaving yourself open to losing everything if they turn nasty.

2

Theories, Choices and Tim Tams

As I mentioned in the introduction, there are two fundamentally different solutions to getting your name onto
as many different deeds for property as possible by the
time you retire. There's the pay-out-each-property-as-you-go
method, which I prefer, and there's the in-debt-to-your-
eyeballs option. But there's also countless variations in
between which may suit you better and which you should
soon be able to design for yourself.

One of the most recent adaptations that's floating
around is the have-your-cake-and-eat-it-too method.

THE HAVE-YOUR-CAKE-AND-EAT-IT-TOO OPTION

This theory is most often put forward by investment
advisors who can't deny that every spare cent you have is
better paid off your non-tax-deductible home loan debt
than it is invested in any scheme (because there's no
investment product yet which can even begin to compete
on an after-tax basis).

But investment advisors understandably need to make
a living. And not every home owner has the discipline,
motivation or patience needed to stick to paying out their
own home quickly. So advisors have come up with this
reasonably compromising proposal of encouraging you to

aim for closer to ten years to pay your house off, and at the same time recommending that you take out loans for investment so you can start your long-term savings sooner and get maximum benefit out of compounding effects over a longer term.

You'll still have reasonably large repayments to make on your home loan to get your total interest debt down from suicidal levels over 30 years to merely horrible to cope with over ten years, but it's not a bad compromise for people who don't mind floating along to a ten-year plan for each set of investments—or who haven't got a complete stranglehold over their budgets yet.

So if you lack faith in your ability to stick to stricter short-term investment and finance goals, then this method can be a great place to start. Because once you're committed to making repayments on investments at the same time as you're managing repayments on your own home, you're at least committed to making a greater effort to work towards your own success. And once you realise how easy your total debt and investment management can be, you can always step up the pace of both. But . . .

The argument for the have-your-cake-and-eat-it-too method can be presented a little deceptively however, because most of the models I've seen that are used to sell this idea are based on the assumptions that:

a) you're already heavily involved in a mortgage that's going to be a real chore to get rid of. (But most mortgages can be paid off MUCH faster by either refinancing them under better conditions or using the loan features—and their loopholes—more efficiently.)

b) you're already getting the best out of your budget that you can. (But I haven't found anyone yet who can't find between $50 and $270 every fortnight extra in their budget—and that's rarely by changing what they buy, just how they pay for things.)

An example of the have-your-cake-and-eat-it-too theory came up recently in the financial pages of a major newspaper. This particular article was written by a leading financial advisor, who I won't name here, as I would hope that the errors and ambiguities in this case were unintentional editing or typing errors. Sadly however, I see these kinds of mistakes all too often, so I'll use this widely published example to demonstrate why every figure on which you're asked to rely your investment future should be double-checked for yourself, BY yourself.

Here's how it went:

If you borrow $150,000 at 6.5% over 30 years, then the minimum monthly repayments will be a flysquat under $950 and you'll pay a grand total of just over $191,300 in interest alone. Pay an extra $170 per fortnight to cut that term back to just 20 years, and your interest will drop by about $73,000 to only $118,000—and since $170 a fortnight isn't too hard to find, you won't have to bother budgeting much to do that. But try cutting your loan back even further to ten years by repaying an extra $755 a month (bringing total monthly repayments to $1703), and the effect of making extra repayments is starting to dwindle away.

Small extra repayments can make a big difference when the term is long, but the effect dwindles away as the term shortens. Once the term is down to about ten years, extra payments don't help much. In this example, there is just $54,000 still to be paid at that last stage. Paying an impossibly high $13,000 a month would cut it back to one year, but you would save only $49,000 in interest.

The first problem is with the basic maths. Check for yourself and see. For instance:

- If you did make those impossibly high repayments of $13,000 a month, you would pay a tad more than $5000 in interest over the one-year term, so to my way of thinking you've saved interest of $191,000 minus $5000, which is $186,000. But this example chooses to compare savings made by paying out a 30-year loan in ten years instead of 20, so it sounds like you're only saving $49,000 in the last ten years.

• After 20 years repaying a 30-year loan, there isn't $54,000 left, there's a tad over $83,000—and that's just the principle. So does that mean there's only $54,000 interest left to pay? Not by my calculator. After paying off a 30-year loan for 20 years, you'll have paid $161,000 in interest, leaving you only $30,300 interest left to pay.

In that case, maybe the article means that you've got $54,000 interest left to repay after paying off a ten-year loan for ten years? Well, it can't be that either. You don't need a calculator to know that if you pay off a ten-year loan over ten years, the balance owing after ten years is zero.

So maybe it means that you have $54,000 interest owing in the last ten years of a 20-year loan? But no, it can't be that either. At the halfway mark of a 20-year loan, you still owe about $98,000 principle plus $36,000—give or take a few hundred—in interest.

What I think it *means* to say is that if you pay out a $150,000 loan out over ten years using repayments of $1700 a month, you'll pay $54,000 in total interest. But if you pay it out in one year, you'll pay only $5000 interest, so the extra $11,300 in repayments per month will save you only $49,000 in interest, and that therefore, the extra stress and effort isn't worth it. Instead, this article suggests you should invest everything you can—over and above those extra repayments that would pay the place off in ten years—into an investment package instead of your mortgage. It omits to say that your budget would be just as strict as paying out this loan in only five to ten years.

It would take a monthly repayment of $2935 to achieve debt freedom in five years, but many double-income couples can afford that without too much trouble once they've got the rest of their finances in order—especially if they haven't started their families yet.

> Yes, extra repayments do have a dwindling effect on your total interest payable as the term of your loan gets shorter. But they have a darn fine impact on your principle and total balance owing—and that effect doesn't dwindle, it just keeps getting better.

> **Handy hint**
> When working out your own have-your-cake-and-eat-it-too plan, also consider the six-, seven- and eight-year options.

MY THEORY EXPLAINED—WITH TIM TAMS

Paying out loans over longer periods than you can actually afford to is just throwing away money. It's almost like paying $800 for a lawn mower that you can buy on sale for $400. Worse than that, it's just fattening your bank's profit margins with your hard-earned cash—a little bit at a time, over the longest period possible.

Let me give you an example that's just crazy enough to show you what I mean.

Example: The chocolate bar version of a Tim Tam at my local store costs $1.80. If I put a deposit of 30 cents down so I can pay the remaining $1.50 off over 30 years at 6.5% interest, then I'll end up paying a total of $3.71 for something that was only worth $1.80. (And that's not even counting mortgage insurance or monthly loan fees, which by themselves could amount to at least $2880.)

If I'm lucky, the value of my precious Tim Tam will go up in value as the packet itself becomes a collector's item.

But I also run the very real risk that my Tim Tam will be worth the same—or even less—than it was when I bought it. So, assuming I couldn't afford more than a 30 cent deposit at the time, I'd rather pay off my Tim Tam over three to five years (if that's all I could afford) and pay only 15 to 26 cents in interest, so the darn thing doesn't cost me more than $2.06 all up. AND I'd also get to invest the whole of every 'repayment' after that if I wanted to— perhaps in Mars Bars or Snakes Alive—for at least 25 to 27 years compounded at an investment interest rate, instead of just whatever smaller investment I can afford while trying to repay my loan over a longer time.

Yes, add zeros onto all of those figures except the monthly fees, and these figures do work precisely the same as for a property loan. So why pay $371,000 for a place if you can afford the repayments to get it for only $206,000? You'll have an extra $165,000 to keep and invest instead of handing it bit by bit to your bank for the rest of your working life.

My golden guide to making profit from property

If you can't sell a house for what you paid for it,
including interest, bank fees, legal charges,
agent fees and improvements, then you haven't
really made a profit at all.

NOTE: I don't count money I get back from tax into the equation, because in the long run—even though I put it towards repayments—I still count that as compensation for years of my time, sweat and worry. Income from the tenants after tax has been deducted also goes towards repayment or gets used for any rates, maintenance, repairs, utilities or other running expenses that aren't paid for directly by tenants. And capital gain from normal inflation in that area is only a bonus after it's kept my dollar up with its buying power.

Aside from the undeniable financial benefits to paying off *all* property promptly, never underestimate the psychological relief of the day you make that last repayment for your home *or* investment property. It's like you're three feet taller, your brain clears of cement and it fills with bubbles of happy gas.

Anyone can learn to live with debt and long-term investment programs. But the stress sets in slowly, and you may never notice the effect it has on you until it's gone—or it's too late.

PERSONAL HOME LOAN OR INVESTMENT PROPERTY—WHICH TO PAY OFF FASTER?

A difficult choice, for which everyone seems to have a different opinion. You already know mine. But settle the matter for your own circumstances by working it out using your own figures:

1. Ring the bank/lender who has the mortgage on your own house and ask how much you have left to repay between now and the end of your loan.
   Write that answer here: $_____.
2. Then ask how much of this is interest. And write that answer here: $_____. (NOTE: None of this interest is tax deductible.)
3. Now divide step 1 by your monthly repayment and this equals how many more repayments you have to make. So you have _____ repayments left.
4. From step 3, you can use a calendar to work out roughly what month and year your last repayment will

be due. (A perpetual or seven-year calendar is best, but any calendar will do, as this step only needs to be rough.) Or you could ask your bank when they expect the last repayment to be. (Sometimes they can tell you easily.) Last repayment due roughly:_____/20____.

5. Now, if you have an existing investment loan (or one that you're considering), ask the same questions for that loan (or look at the projection reports that your advisor should have given you). Then write your answers in a different colour beside the ones above and compare—remembering that this time the interest at step two is FULLY tax deductible.

6. Compare your figures and the answer for your particular situation should 'feel' obvious. NOTE: From a financial point of view for a tax payer the lower your home mortgage, the more tax deductible debt you can afford. But often seeing how long you'll be in debt for the two loans is enough to help you decide which way you want or need to go.

Handy hint: Make only minimum repayments on your investment loan and use any extra income from tenants, mini-tax-refunds or extra contributions out of your own paypacket to get rid of your personal mortgage first.

THE GIST OF NEGATIVE AND POSITIVE GEARING

Gearing sounds like something you'd do to your car, so to make the concept clearer, when you hear the word 'gearing', think 'borrowing'.

Negative gearing is borrowing in such a way that the loan on your investment is so big that interest and other expenses outweigh the income you get from the property (or other investment, like shares). If you add up your income and losses from the property you will get a negative (minus) amount, which you can use as a loss for tax purposes (to lower the amount of tax you have to pay from other income, like wages from your employer).

If your other expenses including interest on your loan is not big enough to outweigh the income you get from the property, it's called *positive gearing*, because you get a positive (plus) amount when you add them together and you will then have some tax to pay on the difference.

Technically, you can still negatively gear a property if you have a small loan but have large expenses—like big depreciation amounts after building warehouses or renovating a house. Just so long as the deductions for expenses are higher than your income from the property, it will be called negative gearing. Even more technically speaking, negative gearing is said to be working when the after-tax cost of an investment is less than its capital gain over the same period. The extent to which that works well for your particular circumstances, depends on:

> In a good market, gearing will increase your returns but it also magnifies losses.

- what your investment expenses are, the biggest chunk of which will be loan interest
- what your personal tax rate is, and that depends on how high your taxable income is, including income from the investment property
- inflation, which for guesstimate purposes, I often use a figure of 3%

It's way too easy to get swept up in the complexities and hype about negative gearing. But the short-term tax benefits of gearing—either positively or negatively— should only be a bonus to helping you get the best out of your investment future—*not* the only reason why you're doing it.

So, ask yourself: if negative gearing didn't exist, would you still be buying that investment for its core potential? Then you'll really know if you're onto the hottest opportunity you can find.

Because simply speaking, the true potential of any gearing can't really be counted until you've taken all purchase costs, running expenses, inflation, capital gains tax and final selling costs into consideration. That's one heck of a calculation and you can get all hot under the collar trying to forecast all of that in advance. So to help you—or perhaps to confuse you more—many advisors have invested in some cracker laptop presentations which have some really great forecast calculators—and often a lot of pretty graphs. But life, inflation and investments can only be forecast *approximately* no matter how fancy your algorithms are.

Yes, many borrowers do depend on negative gearing to stretch budgets so they can actually afford to get into the investments to begin with—and in taking those extra risks, many have made it work quite well. However, your individual circumstances are what's important. Always check with your accountant before attempting any kind of gearing program, no matter how often your investment salesperson tells you that their scheme applies to everyone.

NINE LOOPHOLES

In November 1999, the federal government in Australia moved to crack down on negative gearing for small enterprises especially where directors were earning large incomes from outside sources. As a result, only losses from commercial business activities can be deducted from 'other income'. For example, you can't claim losses from any activities that are run more like hobbies and/or lifestyle choices (eg. unlikely to ever make a profit especially if you earn $40,000 a year or more from an employer or other source). This serves us as a timely reminder that governments can introduce legislation at any time to 'change the rules' even when the principle of negative gearing is still favoured by governments. New Zealand investors should therefore take note of what the Australian government did.

For example, the 1999 crackdown in Australia did not apply to losses that stem from:

1. rental of real estate
2. share investments
3. activities producing a taxable income of more than $20,000 a year.
4. activities employing assets worth $500,000 or more in real property, or $100,000 or more for other assets (except cars)
5. activities that produced taxable income in three of the past five years
6. circumstances outside the control of the taxpayer, such as natural disasters
7. activities with 'a significant commercial purpose or character'
8. carryovers from previous years in which there was no taxable income against which that particular loss could be offset
9. special circumstances that are accepted by the Tax Commissioner

So the most common enterprises to be disadvantaged by the crackdown were mainly small hobby farms or businesses that produced little or no nett income or which are still owned by people who also earn wages over $40,000 a year, and other activities that cannot be dressed up as having any commercial purpose.

The Australian government now uses the rule of thumb that anything producing $20,000 of taxable income, or costing $500,000 to buy in the first place is probably bought as a genuine commercial investment, not simply as a way of dodging tax.

For the New Zealand taxpayer, it is still 'being in the business of renting' which constitutes being able to deduct expenses, whether negatively geared or not.

However, rules are complex and susceptible to change so check with your accountant if you think these guidelines or loopholes may affect you.

Handy hint: The good news for Kiwis interested in making the move to Australia is that property investments in New Zealand can score extra advantages for your wallet. Aside from a tax-deductible trip every year or so to come back and check on your investments, the rental returns are usually higher in NZ, there's no stamp duty on loans (which can add thousands to purchase costs in Australia) and there's no whopping slug for capital gains tax when you sell for a profit, as there is across the pond.

THAT MYSTICAL WORD 'EQUITY'

Equity is the portion of your property's value that you've paid off so far. The rest of your loan shows how much your bank owns. (Sorry to be the bearer of bad tidings, but yes, your bank does own the bit of your home that you haven't paid off yet.) They think of it as a percentage of your property value, but it might be more practical if you think of it as the number of rooms in your house that you've paid off so far.

For example, if you have a mortgage of $250,000 on a $300,000 property, then it's more practical to think in terms that you may own the loo, one bedroom and the hail-battered old garden shed out the back, while the bank

> **Did you know?**
> You can also gain equity by renovating to improve your property's value (eg. adding a shed or landscaped gardens), or by waiting until inflation makes it go up naturally.

owns all the other rooms, plus the driveway and gardens.

Equity is so valuable it makes gold look like beach sand by comparison. I say that because once you have it—either by slogging hard at extra payments yourself, or by applying some of the hints, tips and tricks from either of my first two books to your own mortgage—there will be no shortage of investment schemes, banks or advisors (and their seeing-eye dogs) trying to sucker or seduce it away from you again.

I'm not saying that all remortgaging packages, property investment schemes and negatively-geared shares in property trusts are shonky, however. But I *am* saying that once you've worked hard to gain equity in your own home, don't be too quick to give it up at the first opportunity. Always look for alternative ways of raising your deposits quickly. For instance, you can always trade your flashy car down to a cheaper reliable one, or 'cash-in' your holiday and long-service pay by switching jobs, or make money from your bric-a-brac by holding a garage sale.

ON THE SUBJECT OF VALUATIONS, EQUITY AND ASSUMPTIONS . . .

Consider this: If you can raise the deposit for a rental property WITHOUT 'releasing the equity' from any other property or taking out a second mortgage or bridging loan AND if you can afford the repayments on the new property all by yourself (or with only a small contribution from rental income or tax concessions), then why in the name of the Great Grey Ghost does every bank on the face of the planet seem to leap to the assumption that they should take a valuation over your other property(ies) or first home too?

If you can't see anything wrong with this, then chop up the onions for your gravy, because your duck is ready for roasting.

Why? Because the 'bank'—being a money-making-machine—wants you to put up as much as you can as collateral. They often want repossession power over far more assets than they need, so that if you miss a repayment or three when things get tough, or if the valuations nose-dive, they can repossess all—or any—of your properties that they choose. Don't expect a fair assessment of what needs to be repossessed and what doesn't. The idea of a repossession is THEIR fast recovery—and they'll add whopping repo charges to your list of debts. So if you've mentioned your cars, stockmarket shares or other assets on your loan application, you can often say goodbye to them too if the bank decides to sell you up and doesn't think they'll recoup enough to cover your debt just from hocking all your houses.

MONEY MAKERS, NOT LOSS MAKERS

It's my opinion that investment properties should be just that—*investment* properties. They should be money *makers*, not just tax deductions that you hope will make you a worthwhile capital gain in the long run. Use investment properties as stepping stones to greater wealth. Use them to make money in the short term as well, with tax deductions and long-term capital gain as a bonus. After all, the whole idea of investing in property is to make money, isn't it?

Unfortunately, all you ever hear about in the media or from banks and investment advisers, is that the fastest and easiest way to build a massive property portfolio is by using 'clever' debt management schemes to maximise your tax returns every year. Sure, you get to have your name on multiple property deeds quickly by releasing equity from your home (borrowing against it), but you don't really own any of the properties then. You only own a portion of them—or in the case of interest-only loans, you really only own the *chance* to own them, if you work hard to guarantee raising the capital while you're paying all the interest.

Every fresh investor—and quite a few old hands too—

are bombarded by the concept that getting your tax back every year while you're paying off your portfolio is your biggest goal, but remember that you only get back a portion of your expenses via the tax man. In my experience, you can do at least three times better for yourself in the long run (with only a fraction of the risk) by aiming each time for what you've been brainwashed into thinking is impossible—full ownership.

> The strongest financial position is where
> your investments support themselves
> AND
> provide you with a perpetual income
> so YOU can choose when and how long
> you wish to work.

RELEASING EQUITY TO BORROW FOR LONG-TERM CAPITAL GAIN

What a nice, clean way of saying 'get back deeper in debt if you've been naughty by not saving for your next deposit.' Of course it's a *great idea* to get back some of your EXTRA house repayments *if you have a plan to catch up* again in the next three to five years.

But borrowing against the natural increase in your property value or borrowing back to the full extent of your loan is simply leaping back to financial square one for a few years. So you'd want to make a darn fine return on your investments in that time to catch up to where you were or could have been just by starting a savings/investment plan with shares or even term deposits. (Remembering that your returns have to be big enough to get you ahead as well, which was the purpose of the exercise to begin with.)

'Release the equity,' many advisors will suggest if you haven't got a deposit. 'Why have all that equity sitting in one or two properties, when you could borrow against it and take out interest-only loans to buy *tens* of houses. You could manage investments worth *millions*!' (Speaking cynically for a sec, there's usually a very encouraging-looking smile that goes with that because they get fat commission cheques upon settlement while you have to sweat through years of risk and repayments for a long term gain.)

Whether you release equity for a big deposit or not, carefully study the following points that are all used to calculate capital gain. Because if you do the best you can in each of these areas, you will always stimulate the greatest long-term capital gain possible for that purchase. Remember that currently in New Zealand there is no tax on capital gains. Yahoo!

HOW TO KEEP YOUR NECK SAFE ON THE CHOPPING BLOCK WHEN RELEASING EQUITY

By releasing equity that you've already built up in your assets in order to take out bigger debts, you're just stretching your neck back a little more onto the mortgage chopping block. You're safe so long as the axe doesn't fall. And with luck, patience and a little hard work, you'll do just fine out of the extra investments you just bought.

Remember that commitment to paying loans out over 12 years or more can be chaining you to a day job for the rest of your life, just to stay afloat.

Remember too that the banks get regular market reports on property values in all areas, so be suspicious if your rates go up and then shortly afterwards, you get fresh junk mail offering you free valuations on your property IF you borrow against it to buy more houses.

So yes, release the equity of any EXTRA repayments you've made already on existing loans if you want to use it as a deposit on another property. That way, you'll be no worse off than if you'd made no extra repayments at all. But if you want a safety net in case valuations drop instead of rise, then hog all the natural increase in equity to yourself.

POINTS USED TO WORK OUT CAPITAL GAIN ON ANY PURCHASE

- purchase cost—so the better price you bargain, the greater your initial capital gain
- financing costs including interest, bank fees and charges—so the lower your costs, the greater your gain
- real estate agent fees on buying and selling, and legal fees etc.—ditto
- expenses in improving the property eg. new sheds, fencing, renovations etc.—ditto
- an allowance for inflation as provided by the government for that period—see your tax accountant for details
- any special concession legislated by the government of the day—refer this one to your accountant too
- value of the property in the future when you sell it (so the higher your sale price, the greater your capital gain. Or if you're inheriting it, you may prefer a lower transfer valuation. Speak to your accountant about transfer costs if that applies.)

FOUR GOLDEN RULES TO MAXIMISE YOUR CAPITAL GAIN

From the list above, you should instantly see four golden rules that help you maximise your capital gain on *any* property purchase. Some points you don't have much control over unless you're chairman of the Reserve Bank or a political baby kisser. But others are quite open to manipulation or minimisation, as follows.

Rule #1: Bargain or shop around for a good deal on the purchase price. Not necessarily the cheapest, mind you, just the best value for money. (See page 71 for my favourite 'how to' tips.) For example, you should remember that I've saved between $40,000 to $80,000 on the original listing price of each property so far, just by using my methods of checking 'value for money/true valuation'.

Rule #2: Minimise your loan and finance costs. That means getting the best value interest rate you can and paying it off in the shortest possible timeframe.

For example: A $200,000 property paid off in 25 years at 8% interest will cost you a whopping $263,000 in interest alone PLUS around $2400 in monthly fees (if they're running at $8 a month), making the grand total of repayments over $465,000! Paying it out in ten years will cost you a much smaller $91,200 in interest plus $960 in monthly fees. And working it down to debt-freedom in five years will cost you a relatively meagre $43,300 in interest and only $480 in monthly fees.

Rule #3: Minimise real estate agent fees. *When buying,* do it by purchasing property through your solicitor and/or by bargaining a better sale price. Also, agent fees are usually a percentage of your purchase price, so they go down with every dollar you bargain off the price. *When selling,* minimise costs by selling through agents who don't charge whopping advertising or auction fees. NOTE: Some sole agents only charge for advertising if the property sells.

Rule #4: Minimise expenses for improving the property value by always shopping for value for money when making repairs or improvements. Compare quotes or do-it-yourself wherever possible and practical.

NOTE: In the example in Rule #2 above, I included a costing for monthly fees, mainly because monthly fees are fast becoming an unavoidable fact of banking life. Some banks help you minimise fees if you use their accounts according to the strict methods they recommend. (And of course, each lender has different rules and they all change their guidelines too regularly for me to publish and keep current for you.)

It's interesting to note, however, that on a $200,000 loan, $8 a month in fees is the same as an extra 0.004% in interest. On a $100,000 loan, it's the same as an extra 0.008% interest.

Warning: Wherever monthly fees are brought in AFTER loan repayments have been calculated (or where they get stuck onto existing loans), you MUST increase your monthly repayment enough to cope with it, or else your loan repayment may not be enough to repay the amount you owe from the next month onwards. Slowly but surely you will start slipping further and further behind.

Handy hint: Increase your automatic repayment by the value of your monthly loan fees just to be sure it's done, even if you think you may have done it once before. The worst that can happen is that you'll start making tiny extra repayments that will slowly start getting you ahead.

PLOT YOUR OWN PATH
Now that you understand the theories and choices available, you can give yourself a money makeover to ensure that you're operating all your accounts as efficiently as possible and that everything you're buying or paying subscription to is something that you really need or cherish. Cancel anything that's not and make sure that you're putting money aside every pay for upcoming bills. Then check out any current opportunities for switching loans to take advantage of any special interest rate offers for new loan customers. (Making sure you can get out of it cheaply again if you have to and that it doesn't bite your wallet any worse than normal when your special interest rate period is over.)

Then with your revitalised budget in hand, work out how much you can comfortably afford to make in total loan repayments, including your car, credit cards, home and geared investments (the ones that you've borrowed money to buy). Use that to decide how much you can afford to repay over the period that you would like to do it over. (If you have a company or complicated tax obligations then you should check with your accountant that you're not overlooking anything at this point.) Use a loan calculator or the repayment tables in the back of *Your Mortgage* (or ask your lender for help) to fill out this table as a summary of what you can afford:

If I can afford repayments of	Then these are the size loans I can afford to repay			
	in 3 yrs	in 5 yrs	in 8 yrs	in 10 yrs
$ /Fn				
$ /Fn				
$ /Fn				

Then use this table to help you choose what type of investment property you can afford from those which suit you best before taking the plunge.

There's just two topics we have to cover before that, however: which loan you'll be using and through whom you're going to buy it, as both of these will strongly affect your decisions. So let's start the next chapter with the hardest topic: which loan?

NOTE: Readers of my first two finance books will realise that investors should still be working on a fortnightly basis for all their investment budgets to get the full benefit of 13 repayment months per year instead of 12.

3

Which Loan?
(Shortcuts Through the Maze)

You need to know what type of loan you want before you go property shopping because many of your long-term goals will be affected by the rules you have to follow for the various loans. But first you'll need a few quick definition alerts.

Definition Alerts!

A Principal and Interest loan (P&I Loan) is one of the most commonly available property loans in New Zealand. It's where each monthly repayment gets deducted off whatever the total of your principal and interest comes to for that month.

Daily reducing means that interest is calculated daily, so that whenever you make a repayment, the loan will be reduced by that much, and the next day interest will be calculated on the new lower amount.

Interest-only loan means that you're only repaying the interest on the loan and that you have to save up and pay the lump sum principal to the bank at the end of the loan OR apply to start a new loan when that one ends.

Mortgage offset accounts/revolving credit/ mortgage cruncher accounts all mean basically the same thing—that any money you have in a linked savings account reduces the interest you have to pay on your mortgage. Conditions and packages vary slightly between lenders, and some lenders have a great loophole where you can have more than one linked account at any time (so you can keep holiday, Christmas and other savings safely separate from the account that you raid daily for living expenses). They also usually have a credit card linked to them, but you may not have to use theirs if you have a better deal somewhere else.

NOTE: For three of my first four property purchases, I only ever used a basic no-frills P&I loan. It wasn't until the last few months of my fourth loan that I eventually found a mortgage offset loan (revolving credit loan) that had features which exceeded the traps of using it. They change all the time, but the advanced checklist on page 37 applies to ALL loans for ALL circumstances that I've come across so far. Record your findings on page 236.

Warning: Mortgage offset accounts can be dangerously expensive in the hands of people who have anything less than a tight stranglehold on their budget. In such cases, you still can't beat an almost old-fashioned principal and interest loan (so long as it fits the checklist).

REFINANCING FOR MANY REASONS

Many people seem to refinance these days so they can buy themselves an expensive luxury, like a swimming pool, new car or holiday overseas. Or they refinance so they can fund a business project or a string of investment loans by putting a bigger mortgage on their house.

The idea is always so they'll be better off in the long

run, but how many people ever try to make their business or investments catch up the repayments on their mortgage? Very often therefore, the final result of refinancing is for borrowers to wind up even deeper in debt.

But refinancing can get you out of a hole too. You can refinance to restructure your debt onto a lower interest rate, or to take advantage of new loan offers and make life easier and cheaper in the process. Other times, you may simply need to take drastic steps to rescue your finances so you can start from square one again and move on.

ADVANCED VERSION OF THE PROPERTY LOAN CHECKLIST

Readers of *Your Mortgage* will remember the Property Loan Checklist to help them recognise the five things they need to look for, so they know when they've found a loan that's best suited to paying off their house in five years or less. But financing an investment property may require semi-regular refinancing, whether it's to:

- deliberately manipulate the minimum repayment required
- take advantage of new loan offers
- buy other investments
- restructure your investment debts

The checklist for this book is therefore a little more advanced. (But you can still use it to help find the best loan for the purchase of your own home.)

Loan Checklist
(The advanced version for people who refinance once or more.)

1. It must be daily reducing. (Cash payments must be deducted from the amount owing on the day you

deposit them—or next day at worst, if made by cheque.)

2. It must be able to accept additional payments at any time—whether for a fixed term loan or not.

3. All additional payments must reduce the principal immediately, not treat the principal and interest amounts separately OR have extra payments held for any period.

4. It should have little or no early payout fee. (NOTE: Some lenders make sure their early payout fee is a percentage of the balance owing, so it costs too much for you to leave them and go to another bank again for years. See next page for two radical tips for avoiding these fees if you're already locked in this kind of loan.

5. It should have little or no monthly or ongoing fees, or fees that can be avoided or minimised by opening other savings accounts or term deposits with that bank.

6. It should have zero or close to zero establishment and application fees.

7. It should have no fee for monthly statements.

Optional extras

1. **A mortgage offset or linked savings account** which reduces the amount of interest you have to pay. *Handy hint:* Ask your lender if you can open more than one mortgage offset account with them, so you can keep the money you've put aside for maintaining your investment property separate from your personal income. Even better, you can set up offset accounts for each of your Christmas, holidays, shares savings, home improvements and bill savings, so you don't spend them by accident from your main offset account. Some small businesspeople even 'park' their excess company funds in their personal mortgage

offset account until they pay their company bills each month, even though the fine print in the loan documents usually state specifically that linked accounts should only be for personal use. (So far, lenders seem to be turning a blind eye to this practice and one bank has told me that they won't bother enforcing the rule on their clients, so long as the number of withdrawals per month is kept under the number of extra free withdrawals they are allowed for that account.)

2. **A linked credit card** with a long interest-free period, so you can buy everything from door handles to garages, groceries to holidays on credit, leaving your cash in your offset account for as long as possible every month, before making only one withdrawal at the end of the month to pay your credit card off IN FULL.

Handy hints: The best credit card conditions aren't always offered by the lenders who offer you the best mortgage offset or revolving credit loans. So use the credit card you like at the bank you like and use electronic banking services or telephone banking or direct debits (or walk from one bank to the other once a month, so there's no cheque fees) to shift money from your offset savings account to your credit card, so you still pay it out in FULL each month. Get a credit card with a good rewards scheme, and you'll also get points for freebies with every dollar you spend. (Mine gives me free petrol!)

TWO RADICAL TIPS FOR AVOIDING EXTORTIONATE EARLY PAYOUT FEES

Radical tip 1: If your loan has an early payout fee that's calculated as a portion of the balance owing, then it's often next to extortion to get your large loan switched to another bank. But your new lender wants your business, so the first thing you should try is asking your new lender to help you pay out the old loan by using two cheques over two days, instead of one payment on the day of transfer.

Perhaps the first cheque is from a personal loan or overdraft that they'll extend to you specifically for the purpose of helping you to switch loans over to them. Put simply, you apply for a new mortgage for the full amount of what you owe with the old mortgage. Then you apply for the biggest unsecured personal loan you can from your new lenders, effective from the day before your new mortgage pays out the old one. (If you're lucky, you'll get them to agree to about $100 less than what your old mortgage is.) Then the personal loan gets paid into your old mortgage the day before your new mortgage pays out your old loan. The early payout fee is only calculated on what was owing on the last day of your loan, so it's only a fraction of what it could have been. And then the rest of your new mortgage pays out your personal loan.

Approximate costing: Let's assume your old mortgage is $130,000 and your new lender will extend you an unsecured personal loan of $80,000 until they pay it out with your new mortgage. (Usually, even $80,000 for an unsecured loan is stretching the upper limits of their guidelines a bit, but you can ask.) And then let's assume the interest rate on the personal loan is 14% a year and the early payout fee for your old mortgage is 2.5% of the balance owing, then interest on your personal loan will cost you about $30.70 for the night. But having your personal loan deposited onto your old mortgage the day before your new mortgage pays out the rest will save you an incredibly worthwhile $2000 in payout fees.

NOTE #1: Since the personal loan is really just a paper exercise for your new lender to help them get your new business, I think they'd be rats to charge you set-up fees for it, especially when they know they'll be paying it out in full after only a day. But I'd forgive you for paying them the thirty bucks interest with a smile if they asked. (I'd be grinning too.)

NOTE #2: Early repayment penalty fees are calculated in different ways so it is imperative you check with your lender before taking advantage of Radical tip 1.

Radical tip 2: If your new lender won't or can't come to your party on the above suggestion, you could try doing it yourself with an unsecured overdraft from somewhere else. Choose one without application or set-up fees—like some of the overdrafts offered by credit unions to their members (who usually also loan to close relatives of their members)—and try for their upper unsecured limits of $30,000 to $50,000. Of course, timing will be up to you, so you should probably give yourself an extra day to make sure your electronic transfer request (so there's no cheque fees) will be cleared out of your over-draft and into your old mortgage BEFORE your new mortgage pays it out.

Doing it yourself also means that both your old mortgage and your new mortgage will need a mortgage offset account or other savings account linked to them because someone at one end or the other is going to notice that the loan you need to pay out is thousands less than what the payout cheque has been written for, and they'll automatically look for one of your other accounts in which to deposit the excess. So, if you don't want to delay getting the rest of your money in order to pay out that new overdraft, you'll have to be ready for that.

Approximate costing: If interest rates on the overdraft are 12%, then $50,000 will cost you $16.44 a day. But if the early payout fee is 2.5% of the balance owing, you'll still save an enticing $1250.

NOTE: When applying for your new mortgage or overdraft, you must declare all other loans and debts that you are aware of. But neither your new lender nor your overdraft supplier is likely to believe that you only want the overdraft for a short time or for that single purpose. So be careful that your overdraft application doesn't apply for more than what your income can repay, or else you run the risk of having one or both of your applications rejected when the credit checks are done on you.

INTEREST-ONLY LOANS

I personally don't like these loans and wouldn't normally touch them with a 20-metre power-pole. But if you're absolutely DESPERATE to buy a property and can't afford it any other way, then these loans may be your only reputable choice. A lot of investors these days are using interest-only loans to build their portfolios, and some are succeeding—by luck, guts and tightrope debt/tax management.

> These days, most loan types can be used for most property purchases. Your choice relies more on how much you wish to stretch your buying power than it does on what you're buying. But so long as your loan has the features on the advanced loan checklist, you should do well.

These loans come into their own by allowing you to pre-pay a whole year's worth of interest at any time up to the last day of the financial year. Why would anyone ever want to pre-pay a lump sum of interest to a bank? Well, it gives you a whopping tax deduction in the year that you do it. So if you earn heaps more than you expected, you can buy an investment property at the last minute, get a tax deduction on interest equivalent to owning it for a full year and pay next to no tax at all if the interest bill was big enough. You can't always go on doing that every year though.

What worries me most about these loans, is that some lenders are giving interest-only loans to older people so they can 'buy' their own homes on very low incomes.

But interest-only loans DO NOT pay off the property.

You will NOT own the property at the end of the interest-only period unless you have been ferreting every spare cent you can find into a savings account or other investment and can PAY OUT the purchase price IN FULL out of your own pocket on or before the last day of your interest-only loan.

If you can't, then you have to take ANOTHER loan. But if you can't get a new loan approved, you could be kicked out of your home—or should I say, the bank's home—just like any other tenant who can't afford to pay the rent.

Possible solutions: Reputable lenders can help by making goal accounts compulsory under most circumstances—instead of just recommended—for anyone who takes out an interest-only loan to purchase their own residence. This way, their clients can either pay the place off at the end, or they can use the money so they don't have to take out such a big interest-only loan the next time their loan 'expires'.

Lenders can also help by advertising *loudly* that interest-only loans do not pay off a property. They are—to over-simplify—merely humungous bank fees that you have to pay off over a long time, in exchange for the opportunity to save up and pay cash for your own home, whilst living in it and managing the maintenance of it—free of charge and at your expense—for the bank who owns it in the meantime.

DEPOSITS

I like to consider a deposit made in three stages. There's the deposit you *should* make to the sales agent, the one that you *must* make in order to qualify for a loan from your lender, and the one that you *choose* to make to get yourself financially ahead faster. They do overlap to some extent and they do all add up to the one big deposit that you make—without costing you twice for any part of it. But there are different hints and warnings for each stage which have protected me from shifty vendors, sales agents and lenders, as well as saved me considerable inconvenience and unnecessary expense. Let me explain.

Stage 1: The deposit that you SHOULD make

This deposit can be made to the sales agent in one or two parts. The first part is put down to get the ball rolling. A hundred bucks is often enough for a residential property, or no less than $1000 for a business premises like a warehouse, shop or office. Part two can be made—if required at all—at a time that suits all parties. And unless you're very trusting, not until AFTER the vendor has added their signature to the contract AND the finance for your loan has been approved.

Why? Because larger deposits can be at risk in

> **Did you know?**
> I signed a contract on a property once with nothing more than my $12 of my sanity allowance in my wallet. I handed all my coins over and nipped off to the bank (technically, as a vagrant, because I had less than $2 on me) and I went back later that afternoon with the other $88 in cash to make up an agreed $100. But I got away with it because before leaving, I had worded the contract to say that I would put down a few thousand more as soon as the contract had been signed by all parties.

the hands of shifty agents or vendors, and the interest that the money earns is always better off in your pocket. (NOTE: If the deal falls through due to no fault of yours, then interest from the trust account is supposed to be refunded to you with your deposit. But good luck getting it. Some agents will just tell you there wasn't any.)

Yes, any interest your deposit earns during that time IS supposed to be passed on to the vendor if the deal goes through (or paid to you if it's not), but interest from these trust funds is rarely anything to crow about. Any sane vendor will be more interested in the fattest figure on the contract—the amount they get at settlement—than in the deposit, even if they're being crushed in a rush by

---

Warnings

- Banks usually require total deposits to be 20% of the property price, while building societies and credit unions often accept as low as 5%. So *regardless of who you're borrowing from*, don't tell the agent you have any more than 5% set aside for the price bracket you're looking in, or they may try to convince you to hand it over for their safe-keeping.

- Never discuss your deposit with a sales agent until you're ready to sign the contracts. They may be trained to assume that if it's higher than 10% of the price bracket you're shopping in that you can afford a more expensive property. Of course you can. But it's YOUR choice what price bracket you buy in and what size loan and repayments you wish to commit to.

- If you don't have more than 5% deposit, don't be bullied into over-extending yourself. If you do feel bullied, then SIGN NOTHING without showing your solicitor first, because it's next to impossible for them to help you if you've already given away your signature.

buyers. So long as you've agreed to provide about 5% before settlement, it's usually how much they'll get, how short the contract is and what they get to keep out of the property after settlement that helps them decide who their 'winning buyer' will be.

Stage 2: The deposit that you HAVE to make

This part of your total deposit is to qualify you for your loan. It's enormous, but thankfully it includes the one you should have just made to the sales agent. That shouldn't usually be more than 5%, as just explained. The rest is best given to your solicitor or to your bank, for handing over to the vendor's solicitor directly at settlement.

How much? Well, it used to be that real estate agents would want a 10% deposit as soon as you signed a contract—and some still do. But most reputable agents seem to be happy if you give them enough to cover their commission before settlement, so they don't have to constantly chase the vendor for their money.

Some of the shiftier agents—especially ones that siphon off trust fund interest into their own pockets—will try to goad bigger deposits out of you. Their usual argument is that a larger deposit—up to 10% or more of the offer price—will make your offer more tempting to the vendor. But the vendor won't see one shiny buck of it before settlement because it's parked in 'an independent' trust fund for safe-keeping. (Or in a solicitor's trust fund, if you're buying privately, so you can guarantee getting it back if the deal falls through and it's not your fault.)

As noted, banks usually ask for up to 20% of the property price as a deposit, while building societies and credit unions will often accept as low as 5%. But you should know that any lender can insist on deposits higher than 20%, if they're worried that the property is vacant land or land that's in a difficult re-sale area, in case they have to repossess it and sell you up.

There is one main reason why a lender might request a deposit higher than 20%: if they fear the property isn't worth the full amount you're paying for it. Remember, just because YOU fall in love with a property (or its growth potential), doesn't mean your lender will. The valuation you pay for as part of your application fees will tell them what the property is worth and initially they'll only approve a loan of up to 80% of that amount.

Then they'll either ask you to cough up a deposit big enough to cover the rest of the sale price, or they'll offer to increase your loan and charge you a lump sum mortgage insurance fee, which ensures the bank gets its money back if you renege on your loan repayments later.

If you can't put up the cash to pay for the lump sum mortgage insurance, they may offer to add it to your loan—which sounds like a kind offer, until you work out how much interest you'll be paying them for it over the full term of the loan!

Warning: If your financial institution asks you to pay lump sum mortgage insurance when taking out your loan, make sure the property is worth what they say it is by getting a second valuation done

> **Definition Alert!**
> **Mortgage indemnity insurance**—also known as lender's mortgage insurance—is paid by you, usually as a lump sum when you take out a loan worth more than 80% of the property's real value or sale price. But it protects the lender—NOT you—against financial loss if you renege on your loan. Don't confuse it with mortgage protection insurance, which you pay regularly—sometimes as part of your loan repayment—to protect you by making repayments if you lose your job or get sick, or by paying it out completely if you die or get permanently disabled.

privately. If your second valuation is 80% or more of the contract price, ask your lender to get their valuation checked—providing a copy of yours as evidence. (Ask for a refund as compensation for your extra expense, or at least ask for a discount if there was an error—because all businesses, including valuers, should be responsible for the repercussions of their work. You might not get it, but at least it will put pressure on them to do a better job next time.)

Conditions of payment

You can put other conditions on payment of the deposit —especially if you're paying the vendor close to the price that they're asking. These include holding off on the full deposit until finance is approved, or until certain repairs have been made by the vendor, or until you get confirmation from an independent valuer that the property is worth what you've been told it's worth. You could also hold off on the full deposit until a building inspection has been done to make sure it's structurally sound, or a pest control company has given it the all-clear. These requests can also be negotiable.

Handy hint: To be extra safe, make sure you add a clause —if it's not already there in the standard contract—that ALL parties must initial ALL changes, or the contract shall be considered null and void in all aspects. (Ask your solicitor for the safest wording of this clause for the particular state in which you're buying the property.)

Then, if the vendor doesn't accept any of your terms, they can delete the words they don't like from the contract and initial the changes. The contract will not be a contract until ALL parties have agreed to ALL terms. So the agent will return to you with the contract for your initials (which you don't have to sign unless you agree to the varied terms, because you may wish to renegotiate).

Good real estate agents will make sure that all parties

have initialled all the changes anyway, but you'll sleep better knowing that nobody can change the terms of the contract that bears your signature without your initialled consent.

More handy hints

- If possible, pay your initial deposit by credit card—some agents have the facility available for other purposes, so you can claim your deposit back on your credit card's insurance if anything goes wrong (or get a truckload of award points if all is okay).

- Leave your chequebook at home when you go house-hunting. Some agents say you only look serious if you take it with you. But no sane person I know walks around with their chequebook sticking out anywhere that's obvious—and more importantly, having it with you leaves you vulnerable to swift-talking agents. If you have to go home to get it, at least you've got thinking time to consider if you're being rushed into a sale that doesn't suit you—*and* to remember that you've still got a checklist to go through and more questions to ask.

Stage 3: This is the deposit that you *choose* to make

This deposit is the extra cash you put down in order to make your loan EXACTLY what you choose to afford.

Warning: If you're making an offer that's lower than the vendor's asking price, DO NOT put down more than 10% of the original asking price or it will look like you can afford full price. *Solution:* You can still make a larger deposit to keep your loan down by instructing your bank to draw the extra amount from another account. Or you can give your solicitor a cheque for the extra deposit to hand over at settlement, because as long as the terms of the contract are met, the real estate agent doesn't need to know how big your loan deposit really is.

My solution: When I'm making an offer that I'd like to be accepted without hassle, I put down 4% to 8% as an enticement and tell them that I can't get the rest—although I really want to—until I roll it out of investment, which is always true anyway.

GOLDEN RULE TO FINANCIAL INDEPENDENCE

Just because you CAN afford something, does NOT mean you have to buy it. An investment property should only be a small part of your overall investment portfolio. If you over-stretch your entire investment energies into one property then the same agent who sent you up the creek in a barbed wire canoe will be watching the mortgagee auctions and for-sale ads so they can throw you a lead lifejacket on your way back down the river.

That's when the bidding power is completely in their pockets. They know how much you paid and when, and they know the going rate of interest, so it's a snap to work out (closely enough) how much you owe on the place when it's repossessed or when you're forced to sell. They can be fairly certain that you haven't built up any equity—for two reasons: If you've overextended yourself on a loan then you couldn't have afforded any extra repayments, even if you'd wanted to. And if the place has been—or is close to—being repossessed, then any extra repayments you made have already been played out.

Handy hint

Never tell an agent the true size of your large deposit. Overly keen agents will take it upon themselves to assume that your deposit is 5% to 20% of the highest price you can afford to pay for a property. They're not interested in your potential leveraging power or savings on loan interest and other fees and charges (made by putting down a bigger deposit). All they see is the size of your deposit as a guide to keeping you steered towards the most expensive property you can afford.

4

Real Estate Agent, Investor Scheme or DIY?

When it comes to buying property, you'll find so many people trying to convince you that their service is the best, that your first property purchase can become horribly confusing. And often, just when you think you've found someone you can trust, they leave the industry before you're ready to buy your next property and you have to start your search for assistance all over again the next time you're ready. So in this chapter, I'll be going through the main aspects of choosing your real estate agent, investment advisor or network consultant—or for doing it yourself. Plus I've included a lot of the traps, hints and shortcuts that should make your choices safer, easier and more fun.

THREE TYPES OF AGENT
I've generally found that real estate agents come in three varieties:

1. The slick talkers who'd sell their own children if they could get a good price for them. (No refunds provided, of course.)
2. The honest schmoes who just want to put a meal on the family table without hurting anyone else in the

process. (These poor guys and gals have a fast burn-out rate, often because of the stress, odd hours and unreliable income—which is one reason why the real estate industry has such a high staff turnover.)
3. Then there's the hardened schmoes who are honest enough to keep a good reputation but hardened enough to insist on a fair middle ground price that's not too bad for all parties.

The slick talkers are excellent fun to play with. (Or they were before my first book became a bestseller. Now they usually recognise me and 'play nice'.) But you can still have fun with them as a way of learning all the latest sales pitches.

Don't go unless you're feeling in complete control, of course. And when you do, go hunting for these agents at many of the disreputable agencies or even at a few of the reputable ones known for bragging about their high sales turnovers.

Begin your learning game by wearing casual clothes and looking at the pictures in their windows on one of your afternoons off work. Then you take out your invisible buzz-phrase bingo card and see how many cliché sales pitches they throw at you in one conversation.

> **Kids and investments**
> It's a great growth experience for your kids to be involved in the purchase process of ANY investment, including shares and property. But do the shortlisting without them. Only take them to the second viewings of property so they don't get bored or overawed. Then ask them for their opinions, because they'll often pick up things that you won't. Even a three-year-old can give you insightful and responsible answers from their shorter, more innocent and less stressed point of view.

Buzz-word phrases usually start with: You'll have to be quick because blah blah; or the last property we had as good as this one sold in blah blah; or I know this really great property that hasn't been listed yet, but blah blah. Obviously, you can make house-hunting a lot more fun for you and your partner if you exchange a wicked glance behind the sales person's back every time you hear one of these. Doing it may be childishly cheeky, but at least it helps keep you alert to buyer's hype, so you're less likely to be talked into a deal that you'll regret later.

CHOOSING YOUR AGENT—FOR BUYING

If you're going to build an investment portfolio with more than one property in it, save yourself time and convenience by finding an agent or two now with whom you feel comfortable. Ask your friends and workmates about their experiences with local agents—or check your *Yellow Pages*—and visit their shop window where a choice of their property listings with photos are displayed. Remember that these ads are only a small portion of what they have available, so even if you don't see anything you like, if they've been recommended by someone else, go in to ask them a few questions—or call later, if you prefer.

Warning: The agent you use to BUY property is not always the best agent to use when you SELL. (See also *Choosing your agent for selling* on page 188.)

Questions to ask

- *Are you paid by commission only, or do you get a salary with bonuses for any sales you make?* Some agents get paid commission based on how many sales they make that month, or how much their sales add up to that month, or sometimes on each sale. So I ask this question because

I've found that agents who are paid only—or mostly—by commission are more likely to be pushy, grumpy or edgy. Remember, agents don't usually get paid commissions until settlement, so the agent who makes your sale will have to wait until at least then to get paid; and even then, their office managers are likely to delay payment so they can take their bite of the cherry too. And since I like to buy properties on a long contract, I don't want my real estate agent disadvantaged by helping me to get the conditions I want if I can help it.

- *Do you use a standard contract provided by the Real Estate Institute?* I ask this one because representatives from the law and real estate industries have come together to draw up a contract which is the fairest to all parties. It's a standard contract, but agents can still hand-write any extra clauses or changes you request onto it, before you sign it. Most of them are familiar with wording required for the most common 'popular requests'. But if you're unsure on the wording for any special request, ask your solicitor to provide exact wording of any extra clauses you want, so your agent can add it to the contract BEFORE you scratch your signature on it. NOTE: Just because you add a clause doesn't mean the vendor has to agree to it. They can negotiate your offer simply by crossing out or changing the new clause and asking you to initial the changes before they initial it too.

- *May I take my car?* I don't really care if I follow the agent's car, or have them sitting in my front passenger seat pointing the way. I make the request because they have Buckley's chance of hijacking me to every lemon property on their books if I'm behind the wheel—and because the extra kilometres in my vehicle logbook increase the tax deductible percentage of my car's annual vehicle expenses. (It also helps me to find the place again, rather than getting distracted by conversation or scenery on the way, which I'm otherwise prone to do.)

Since there's no need to pay the agent any fee to find a property to purchase, there should be no need to discuss payment with them at this stage. But if they do try to convince you to pay for hiring them to shop for the best property—or for providing any other service for that matter—then go somewhere else, or contact your solicitor or the Real Estate Institute of New Zealand to see if that practice is currently acceptable. If not, I'd report the agents immediately to the REINZ and to the Ministry of Consumer Affairs providing full details. (See page 234–235 for important contact numbers.)

NOTE: It is possible to hire a real estate agent to bid for you at an auction held by a rival agent. But unless you trust your agent implicitly AND doubt your own abilities, then you're probably only spending money that you don't have to. (Every dollar you pay to an agent like this is really two dollars they'll have to bargain off the price to make it worth your while.)

HANDY TIPS FOR TAMING YOUR REAL ESTATE AGENT

Real estate agents don't really work for you, the buyer, they work for the vendors, the people selling the place. Agents—even the reputable ones—stay in business by seeking out a monthly balance between selling as many properties as they can, and selling properties for as much as they can.

The fact that they try to build a trusting relationship with you, the buyer,

> **Handy hint**
>
> Agents often suffer a lot of pressure from their bosses in the office to make a sale. So get your agent out of the office and away from other agents to give them an opportunity to be relaxed and honest about the properties they're showing you.

is because they know that most people who buy also eventually sell, and that investors who buy one property may be looking for a second one in six or twelve months' time. So they need to look after you to some extent to attract your repeat business. (And to get you recommending them to all your friends.)

But you can encourage them to take extra good care of you by following a few basic common courtesies and practical tips:

- phone for an appointment at a time when they're not normally very busy
- give them clear guidelines on what you want
- be punctual and organised
- give them feedback on each place you see to help them think of others which may interest you

Making your appointment
A real estate agent's worst nightmare (or their dream, depending on how honest they are) is someone who walks in off the street on their busiest Saturday morning and says, 'Gee, I think I want to buy a house, but I'm not sure what I want and I don't care where it is, so show me the lot, hey?'

What an excellent way to paint the word *sucker* on your head. You'll be pointed to their shop window to choose a few pics that interest you. Then on the way to inspect them, you'll get dragged off to a dozen lemons so that by the time you get to the houses you wanted to see, you'll be easy to convince that you're looking at a bargain, when you're really just looking at the property they want to sell you.

NOTE: It's fine to go window shopping over a couple of weeks or weekends beforehand, but try not to get sucked into conversation with an agent at this stage. The best properties are usually in their filing cabinets, not always in their windows, but you can waste a lot of time in agencies looking at listings—or worse, get suckered into looking at properties you don't want—if you wander in off the street.

When making your appointment by phone

- Give them a list of at least five things you are looking for in a property.
- Ask them to show you the top five to ten property listings they have that suit your description plus two others they think are bargains and tell them they only have you for three to five hours, after which you'll be off to the next agent to do the same with them.

HOW MANY REAL ESTATE AGENTS SHOULD YOU USE?

I like to look in about five to ten agency windows over a period of a few months before going property hunting seriously, but I usually only speak to about three or four agents, which usually include:

- the agent I use most in that area
- another reputable one or two with the most interesting or honestly presented window displays
- one of the 'questionable' agents—who one day must surely list a bargain in time for me to look at instead of telling me: 'Oh gosh, sorry, ma'am. You just missed that one. It went under contract yesterday. But we have this other one . . .'

Then I usually spend car-time with only two or three agents—and unless I feel like playing, they're always reputable.

Be suspicious if . . .
- The most appealing bargain is the second or third last one you see for the day, after being dragged to lemon after lemon after lemon. Chances are you've been shown properties in a particular order to help convince you that you're looking at their bargain. Often the last property of the day is another lemon— if only to reinforce the idea that you did see a few 'good' ones in your adventurous travels.
- Also be suspicious if the agent gets messages every five minutes on his mobile phone from another agent back at the office, who's warning you that they have someone else sitting down to sign a contract on the place right now, so you'd better hurry and make a higher offer if you really want it. (Don't laugh. One agency actually tried that one on me.)

Did you know?

The old sales pitch 'You don't have to like a property to buy it for investment, because you're not the person who has to live in it' is a lorry-load of codswallop.

If it looks like a rat's nest, smells liks a rat's nest or has rat's nests for neighbours, then the only tenants you'll be able to attract to the place will be rats. When you're buying a property for investment, imagine you're buying a home for a best friend that you haven't met yet—even if you never intend to meet your tenants-to-be.

SALES COMMISSIONS

Conditions for commissions to real estate agents upon sale of a property may vary because in many areas you're now allowed to negotiate the fees involved.

Commissions are technically paid by the vendor—not

you as the buyer—but since you pay a deposit to the agent, and the agent deducts their fee before forwarding the balance after settlement, the money actually goes straight from your hands to the agent's, without the vendor even smelling it.

RESPECTING YOUR AGENT'S EXPERIENCE

After viewing a number of properties and shortlisting a few, don't be afraid to ask your agent's opinion. Because once they're fairly certain of getting a sale out of you, a decent agent will always give you their best guess at which property they think will have better potential for rental income and a quick resale. Just don't rely on that advice completely unless it's backed up by independent sources.

INVESTMENT PROPERTY NETWORKS, CLUBS AND SUPPORT GROUPS

If you're nervous about becoming a landlord then these newcomers to the investment property scene can be appealing. Monthly club meetings offer a place where like-minded investors can get together and compare experiences. They also have newsletters which can keep you updated on industry changes. Some provide services where they 'bulk buy' properties so you can get them at cheaper rates IF you buy through them. Others help you find property managers and loans as well.

But getting all your services in the one place leaves you vulnerable to rip-offs. Beware of groups being used as fronts for dubious property developers who are just selling properties off the plans of their sister companies. Beware of groups that herd members to the same loans or managers despite your best judgement or reported problems. And avoid groups that make you feel like an outsider, or that you're missing out if you're not doing the same as everyone else in the group. (See also Chapter 10: Managing the Place, and Real Questions Answered.)

DIY PURCHASING

Having read this far, you'll realise now that the biggest traps in buying an investment property on your own can include falling foul of agents who may want their commissions paid by vendors despite your private purchase, and lenders setting up your loan under conditions that drain your pocket dry over the longest possible time.

As a buyer—whether you go through an agent or not—it's also wise to make sure that:

- deposits are receipted properly and held in trust by a solicitor until settlement
- the property description has the correct lot and registered plan reference numbers on all documents including rates notices, certificates of title, purchase contracts and loan agreements
- insurance is arranged on all buildings and contents (floor tiles, curtains, ovens, plumbed-in refrigerators etc)
- the vendor has arranged for the gas and electricity meters to be read and a final account issued before settlement
- that corner markers are where the surveyor's report says they should be. (Sometimes errors are obvious. Maps are viewable online for casual viewers through Landonline for a small fee: www.landonline.govt.nz)
- that you will only pay rates upon settlement for the portion of the year that you'll own the property
- that your Will is updated to include inheritance instructions for the new property
- that the property has been vacated properly before settlement with nothing taken 'by accident' that was included in the sale contract
- that registration of the transfer of mortgage is completed by your lender who holds the title deed to the property until your debt is fully repaid

- that all property searches are done thoroughly by your solicitor, or by yourself as follows:
  - Titles Office, to ensure there's nothing amiss with the transfer of the title deeds and to get a copy of the plan and deed.
  - Local Council, to ensure rates are fully paid, everything that should have council approval does and there are no highways planned for the backyard.
  - Local councils can also supply you with a Land Information Memorandum (LIM) which provides the following important info, usually within 10 working days after receipt of your application:
    — details of any special features (eg. potential for erosion, subsidence, flooding, noxious weeds or possible soil contaminants from previous land usage)
    — details of stormwater and sewage drains
    — details of any current (and previous) permissions granted or warning notices issued for the property by council
    — zoning details, including any restrictions for the land use
    — any other information that the council thinks relevant

Yes, there is usually a fee associated with your application for a LIM—and fees between councils can vary—so only request these details for a property that makes your final shortlisting. In the meantime, don't be afraid to ask the vendors of any property that deserves a serious second look if they'd be willing to provide you with a photocopy of any LIMs they have from when they were buying the place. It never hurts to ask.

NOTE: At the time this book went to print, you could still get FREE contaminated land searches done through

Environment Canterbury (PO Box 345 Christchurch, Phone (03) 365 3828 or 0800 EC INFO Fax (03) 365 3194 or website: www.ecan.govt.nz/About-Us/LIR/LIR.asp). Information about contaminated lands is still being gathered and researched, however, so there's no guarantee yet that the database is complete. You can check them out and make inquiries online through their LIRs (Land Information Requests). Please don't over-use or abuse this free service, however, or they won't be able to keep it free for us for long.

IMPORTANT

Fax or email your solicitor AND your tender two days before settlement to make sure they're all ready for it. Then ask them to fax or email their reply in writing so you can hold them accountable for any big fees or losses you make if they weren't ready and miss settlement. (As too many do.)

5

Which Property?

WHERE TO START?

How do you know what kind of property to invest in when there are so many choices and so many complications that can affect the forecasts and performance of each? Since money is only part of your end goal—security and enjoyment being the other factors—I think comfort and enjoyment should be major factors in your initial decisions too.

For example, if you've been forking out rent to a landlord for years, you'll probably get a real thrill in choosing a house or unit as your investment, so you can enjoy someone else having to pay rent money to you for a change. If you've lived in flats—and have a deposit or income to support the bigger loan—you may prefer to try for a block of flats. If you've always spent holidays at the coast in a rental home, you might prefer to try for one of those. Or if you've been raised in a family of tradesmen, you might prefer a big warehouse that you can partition and sub-lease to multiple industry-related businesses. (For example, if you have a mechanical repair shop, you might use one quarter of the industrial building for yourself, and lease other sections to mower or boat repairers, or maybe a panel beater, a spare parts depot and perhaps even a used car-lot—making it like a one-stop shopping centre specific to the trade of your choice.)

Once personal choice has narrowed your field of options, let your comfort zone guide you a little further. Why get nervous about missing out on a 'fantastic opportunity' in Queenstown if it's personally important that you can drive past the place now and then, just to make sure it's still there?

Then use your financial situation to help you weed out more opportunities from the ones available. Remember, opportunity is everywhere. By this stage, it shouldn't concern you that you'll always have to bypass many to choose only one. *Don't let it worry you.* If you really want a block of flats but can't afford the much bigger loan, then just start with smaller properties as stepping stones to get what you want—and think of it as a bit like a landlord's apprenticeship.

In cities like Auckland and Wellington where even unit prices have hypertrophied, get cheeky. Buy in the provinces, so you get cheaper homes in other cities—and still get great capital growth, not to mention tax deductible airfares, car hire and accommodation to go and check on them once a year.

Or if you're renting, you could look for a friend who's also sick of the rent cycle and see if you can each buy an investment house to rent to each other. If the arrangement suits you, you'll get all the benefits of negative gearing, as well as being able to set the amount of rent you pay by negotiating that your friend has to pay roughly the same amount of rent as you. (There are no set laws about this, but rent levels should still be close to market rates so you're keeping everything honest and 'above-board' for the Inland Revenue. This is not to say the Inland Revenue will accept that both of you are actually in the 'business of renting', unless you're saving up for or buying other investment properties as well.) You'll also be guaranteed good tenants by doing this because you'll be living in your tenant's investment property.

You could also consider buying a holiday home in a tourist centre so you can rent it out to holiday-makers when you're not using it yourself, or maybe move into it yourself in a few years' time when you retire or start your family. But aside from the fact that tourist-tenants will be in party mode from the second they walk in to the second they leave, there will be other downsides to this choice. For example, there are limits to the amount of interest and expenses you can claim each year against tax. Plus all the furniture in the house will be yours, so there will be greater risk of things disappearing. (And insurance premiums and excesses for contents left unattended like this are never friendly.) Plus the greater risk of vacant periods between tenants—especially in the off-season— means you'll also need to have a back-up fund available to help make repayments when the property isn't earning anything.

But that still leaves you with a wide choice of exciting properties to choose from—even once you've been able to narrow your selection down to a certain category. So to help you find that one raw gem amongst the others, you need to be able to create a shortlist. And to do this, a quick and easy checklist and scoring system is going to come in very handy.

YOUR INVESTMENT PROPERTY CHECKLIST

If you flip over a few pages to the end of this chapter, you'll see a checklist I use whenever I'm scoping a potential purchase so I remember to check everything the first time round. These checklists have saved me stacks of time and double-tripping, not to mention thousands of dollars by spotting problems BEFORE they become mine.

> **To use the checklists properly you will need:**
> A clipboard with pen, binoculars, fridge magnet and a small loaded stapler, sunglasses and comfortable shoes.

Handy hints to using the checklist

- **Get professional.** Run off one copy of this instruction page plus lots of copies of the checklist—one for each property you've organised to see (with three spares for properties you might look at if you've got time).
- **Attach them to a clipboard** that has a reliable pen attached by string so you can't lose it.
- **Wear sunglasses** for looking up at gutters, power connections, tall garden trees etc. (looking for suicidal branches that are just dying to attack the roof).
- **Wear comfortable clothes** with shoes that are easy to slip on and off at front doors.
- **Take binoculars** if possible for checking out condition of roof screws or tiles, second storey eaves or high brickwork and the source of rising pollution in any views.
- **Check off each section** of the checklist (in no particular order, using the stapler to attach maps etc.).
- **Discuss each rating with your partner** in the car afterwards. (Sticking to this topic also helps to avoid being drawn into talk about finance and prices by your agent.)
- **Ensure your agent is aware of how you feel** about each point, so they may vary their choice of other properties to show you if necessary without wasting your time. (Sometimes, talk of one property can remind them of another that may be coming up soon for sale.)

MY VERSION OF THE 3 PS

You often hear people say that the three Ps you need to look for when shortlisting a property are: position, position, position. But that's not very helpful, so I prefer

BEWARE: Do NOT discuss price negotiation until AFTER you've finished your investigation. At this stage, you only need to know if the price is negotiable or firm. Repeated attempts by agents to discuss deposits or prices on the day that you look at a property is the surest sign that you're being bullied or swindled—no matter how kind or big their smile is when they do it.

to think of them as position, popularity and physical traits. And I've split up the checklist into those three main categories to help keep everything organised. I've also repeated a few of the following key points on the checklist so you have convenient reminders with you when you go property-shopping.

Position: The property's proximity to services, views, industry, schools and shops means convenience and quality of lifestyle for your tenants. So make it easy for tenants to love your house by choosing a nice one in a nice place. Have a quick look at the first page of the checklist and you'll see what I'm talking about.

Popularity: Properties with popularity attract the best tenants, have the shortest empty periods between tenants, sell faster and provide the best capital growth, even in the short term. Popular properties can be expensive, while properties with potential for popularity provide the best bargains in the medium to long term. Luckily for small investors, all of these points can be verified by knowing what to ask or look for. They're all listed thoroughly in the checklist, but here are some that need a little more explanation:

- Capital growth for the area in the last year: Your real estate agent can show you itemised annual sales reports for each suburb so you can compare how a particular property or area fared against the others. Verify that the reports haven't been tampered with by jotting down a few details or getting photocopies of a few sample pages to check against itemised reports from other agents, whose reports should include details of the same properties sold over the same period if they're for the same area. Don't sweat over any minor variations though. This isn't rocket science. You're just looking for rough trends that the area you're looking at is currently a little slow for no apparent reason.

- Standard of street appeal of neighbouring houses: Remember, if you buy a hole in a rat's nest, you'll only attract more rats. But neat gardens and neat homes usually indicate a quieter neighbourhood, which usually means happier tenants, which means less stress on your investment.

- How far away are industrial estates/military bases/large government department offices for a strong potential job market for your tenants?

- How far is it from hospitals or ambulance? In emergencies, these services come to you. But older tenants, asthmatics or younger parents with little kids will appreciate knowing that help is only a few seconds away. It's also a little-known fact that ambulance subscribers, especially in outer suburbs or rural areas, can get free medical attention to minor cuts and major splinters—including bandaging—heaps faster than they'd get at their local hospital or GP. Just pull up and ask for help from the medic on duty. They usually have spare rooms set up with much comfier chairs than your local doctor's examination beds.

- Has approval been granted for constructing a shopping centre nearby? NOTE: Be very wary of any casual comments along the lines of: 'Woolworths is coming soon.' I know at least one suburb where real estate agents have been brandishing that line for over twenty years. And despite the reputable newspaper clippings that back up their story, no major shopping chain has ever followed through, leaving housing developments floundering in the financial back-blocks. Look instead for cleared acreage with approval notices posted on pickets asking residents to declare any objections before constructions begin. Or ring the council to verify that approval has been granted and ask for construction dates. If you can't find evidence, then shelve the fairy story with all the others, because even though men in fashionable suits may have been spotted checking out real estate in the area, it means nothing until they put their money where their shoes went.

- TV reception: It's one of those things that almost nobody thinks about, but few things annoy tenants more than if they can't get a clear image of their favourite TV shows. Ask how many channels the house gets. Is the aerial in good condition and how is reception quality? To verify, ask owners to turn on their TVs or ask neighbours about any glitches during the day or night. (Do planes fly over and turn everyone on TV green? Does the guy in the next street play with his arc welder or wide-band radio until three in the morning?)

- Pay TV: Have lines been laid to the house or is there a satellite dish? Is everything in full working order? (And later—if the house makes it onto your shortlist—you can ask if there are any special instructions for contract renewal or caring for the dish or its connections.)

- Is there an extra phone line connection to the house for internet or dedicated business lines? This one can be tricky. A house that comes pre-wired for a second phone line can be worthwhile rating a little higher on your checklist, because it's a lot more expensive to put in an extra line later. However, tenants pay for the line rental and the extra cost could be a turn-off for tenants who won't use it. You may have to advertise it as 'second line available' and disconnect it at your expense for tenants who don't want to use it.

- Is there easy access for a removal truck to back up and shift around full-sized wardrobes, refrigerator and mattresses? Some of the better and more experienced tenants may choose a smaller, practical home over a flashier one because they need easy access for getting their larger furniture in and out without damaging it. Experienced tenants know that walls always get bumped and floors scraped, no matter how careful they try to be. That makes it expensive for them in two ways—excess wear'n'tear on their own furniture, plus the risk of losing chunks out of their rental bond to reimburse the landlord for repairs.

  You should be looking for everything in a house that good tenants will be: no paving where trucks have to back in, no droopy trees or low-hanging power lines for them to drive under, no soggy garden beds to bog down in, and no winding stairwells or narrow doorways to navigate.

Handy hint: Better access may be possible if the garden or paving is rearranged. If so, take a note of that so you can negotiate for a longer contract or cheaper sale price and make sure all work's completed BEFORE settlement.

Physical traits: Investment properties not only need to look good, they have to stay looking good for the lowest possible maintenance costs over the longest possible time. But getting dragged from one property to another by agents all week means you'll often overlook a lot of details that could cost you big bucks in the long term. So section three of the checklist should help to keep your mind on the job for each property that sparks your interest.

HOW MUCH IS IT REALLY WORTH?

If you've already figured out how to work this out from the 3Ps above—or if you've read my first book—then you can skip this bit. But for anyone who's a bit unsure, here's a quick run-down on the two methods I use to work out a property's value. I do both so that one cross-checks the other, and yes, it does work just about everywhere, even in Auckland and Wellington, where house prices often look like the devil's own extortion fees.

Method 1: Get the unimproved valuation of the land from the last rates notice. Then add on the estimated worth of the house, garden, driveway, clothesline and fencing. Onto that, add rough approximations of any special features that most people would like; for example spas, in-floor safes, security systems or proximity to shops, public transport and facilities (using fair approximations of what those special features may be worth to you). Then deduct any amount for repairs needed, as well as approximations for replacement or removal of any 'special taste' features (eg. woolly walls, castle spires or thorny hedges).

NOTES: Photocopies of rates notices can be obtained from the current owner through the real estate agent. (The agent usually gets a copy as part of their verification that the person who listed the property is legally able to list it for sale, and as confirmation that the 'real property description' identifies the precise property that is to be transferred on the contract from one person to another.)

House valuations can be worked out roughly from your last weekend newspapers. Look at the floor plans advertised by builders of new homes to see how much a similar-sized house costs to build these days. If the house you want to buy is fairly new then use the builder's price plus about 10%—not for GST, but for carpets, flyscreens, floor-tiles outside wet areas and curtains etc., which are rarely included in the builders' starting-from price. If the house is over seven years old then the builders' basic price for floor plans (including GST) is usually close to the price of an older home after depreciation and fair wear and tear— at least for this purpose. (The only exception might be a 'handyman's dream', which is often a landlord's nightmare. Perhaps you'd buy a handyman's dream to renovate and resell, not for tenants.)

Method 2: Compare prices with similar properties listed with other real estate agencies. Some agents are prepared to show you computer print-outs or onscreen records of recent sales in areas close to where you're looking. They pay for subscription to these to help them stay on top of what's happening in the market, but some agents are happy to share the information—at a glance anyway—with buyers who are serious about buying their next property soon. Also compare similar properties that are listed with other agencies (or read on for internet tips).

Did you know?

I often see houses advertised for one price at one agency, and up to $10,000 less at an agency down the street—or on the next page of a property guide. And it's rarely a deliberate rip-off at the dearer agency. Sometimes the vendor may have dropped the price and not told their other agent before their advertising deadline. Or the vendor may have been convinced to try dropping their price at one agency, while secretly hoping to get their full price through another.

BUYING OR SELLING ON THE INTERNET

For a long time, listing and shopping for real estate on the net had limited success. But with more New Zealanders logging on every year and with transmission speeds, websites and database management evolving all the time, listing, short-listing and virtual real estate tours are finally starting to find their feet.

Many real estate agents now offer internet listing as a feature of their services. Some list your property for free on their own websites, others pass on a fee for listing it on larger databases alongside other agents. The databases are usually free for buyers or prospective tenants to browse. They may also let private vendors list properties for sale alongside agented properties, but the fee will be higher for you than for agents, who get a discount and password to keep listings updated by themselves.

Handy hints

- If you don't have internet access, log on to real estate websites using free or low cost time at local libraries or bookstores that host internet cafes.
- Look for websites with thumbnail pics (small images of the house) that load quickly, but which can be enlarged if you choose, by double-clicking on them.
- Beware of websites charging over $50/month if they're bragging about phenomenal hit rates (visitors to their site per month) and don't have either evidence to substantiate their claim, or a very popular company that links to them from their homepage. (A homepage is the first 'page' you see when a company's website loads on your screen.)
- Try www.realenz.co.nz and www.open2view.co.nz to access a good selection of listings, plus up-to-date interest rate information.
- Check out my website www.anitabell.com for a free link

to a calculator which helps you figure out if it's better for you to rent or buy in the circumstances.

MAKING YOUR OFFER

Once you've chosen the property you want from your shortlist, you're ready to make your offer. You'll already have a feel for whether it's a bargain or not. But now it's time to put figures to your feelings. DON'T just take off a few thousand and ask the agent if the vendor will accept that. You could be missing out on bigger savings which multiply to a small fortune over the full term of your loan. Instead, roughly work out how much the property is really worth using either of the methods just explained and start your negotiations from there.

If the asking price is already below what you calculate it to be worth, you'll know in advance that you'll have trouble getting the vendor to agree to an even lower price. (Try asking for a drop in price that's just enough to cover your legal fees, but be prepared for a knock-back.) If, however, you work out that the vendor wants much more than you can justify, your calculation gives you the best place from which to start negotiating. This is the best time to go ahead and ask for those few thousand dollars off.

Handy hint #1: If your offer is a LOT lower than the asking price—say $10,000 to $80,000 less—then prepare for rejection by telling your agent that you can justify the price if the vendor wishes to negotiate from there. As a last resort, you can write out your offer neatly and ask the sales agent to present your calculations to the vendor with a signed contract.

Handy hint #2: Add a note saying that you believe your offer is calculated as fairly as possible and has been rounded off to your satisfaction; so while negotiation is invited if there are obvious errors or oversights, quibbling over every dollar is not.

Warning #1: If the agent seems upset or tries to bully you into a higher price without being able to correct any of your calculations fairly, then there could be something fishy in Agentsville. Tell them you need to think about it for a day and then use that day—or two—to pop a copy of your offer into the current owner's mailbox, with a note politely explaining that the agent did not wish to make this offer on your behalf.

Ask them for their feedback—to you directly—before reconsidering your first offer, and ask if they have another agent—either at the same agency or with another agency— with whom they would prefer you to deal. It's possible that the sales agent who introduced you to the house is not the agent who listed it for the owners.

But if you receive no reply from the owners, try contacting the agency again on a day that your first agent is having their rostered days off and ask if someone else can help you close the deal by getting a contract offer to the vendor immediately. (NOTE: Switching agents within the same agency is awkward, but legally okay, if you do it through the right channels and for good reason. Switching agencies, however—or trying to finish the deal as a private sale—can get either you or the vendor or both sued by the agent, depending on the circumstances.)

Warning #2: If your offer is much lower than what the agent was hoping to sell it for, and if they're the slightest bit shifty, you'll never know if your offer was accepted. You'll be told that another buyer slipped in a contract ahead of you and you missed out, or that your offer was rejected, or the property was withdrawn from sale. What you won't be told, is that the new owner is the real estate agent, or one of their friends or relatives—or worse—a shelf company owned by the agent who bought it, knowing they could sell it to you or somebody else for a whopping profit.

To avoid being gazumped like this, try making an

appointment with the vendor on site BEFORE telling any-one you want to buy the place so you can ask the real owner some of your questions from the checklist. Make an appoint-ment for a second visit if you have to—preferably with the sales agent present so they know you're playing fair.

If the vendor won't meet with you, ask the agent for a photocopy of the last rates notice. The name on it should be exactly the same as the vendor's name on the contract.

Did you know?

A vacant block of land near me had a cardboard sign tacked to a tree for 11 months that said: 'For sale. Town water. $53,000 phone owner 5427 XXXX' Every now and then the owner came along and went over the writing again in black felt-pen. Then shortly after a heavy rain storm, a passerby in a red car stopped to read the sign. He was back later that day to meet the owner and seemed considerably interested. And although he wouldn't commit, he wouldn't leave either, so the owner asked him what the problem was.

'Well, you want 88 grand for the place,' said the buyer, pointing to the sign where 53 had turned to 88 after the rain. 'But I haven't got a deposit big enough for that. You'll have to take $73,000, and that's that.'

'Yeah, okay,' said the vendor, after a moment of stunned silence. 'I guess I could do that.' And he did.

Moral of the story: Always ask for the sale or starting price. Be wary of volunteering it.

Epilogue: I heard that buyer in the local service station four months later, still boasting about the fantastic deal he got in bargaining $15K off his block in one breath . . . So I guess no-one else in the area has had the heart to break it to him yet either.

If it's any different DO NOT SIGN THE CONTRACT YET. Tell the agent or vendor that you need to show the document to your solicitor before signing it—which is a reasonable request anyway. Then immediately report your suspicions to the REINZ or the Ministry of Consumer Affairs (contact details on p. 234–235) and possibly also to your solicitor and to your local police if necessary.

HINTS FOR INTER-PROVINCIAL BUYERS
Many buyers from southern provinces moving north, or even from city areas moving out to country areas are putting themselves at risk of rip-offs by failing to study the local market thoroughly BEFORE getting on a plane or going for that long drive to look around.

Solution: Use the *Yellow Pages* to look up phone numbers for 5 to 20 real estate agents in the area that you are interested in at least two months before you book those plane tickets. (Your local post office keeps public copies of the *Yellow Pages* for all areas in New Zealand or check out their website at www.yellowpages.co.nz). Then contact the agents to get a copy of their free property guides posted to you. Give them your maiden name or ask them to send it to your parents-in-law's address, so they don't recognise your name so easily when you eventually show up. (Some agents keep a list of the names to whom they send property guides, so they recognise a softer target when you walk in.)

Warning: Never tell a real estate agent that you live in another province or country to the property you're buying, if you can help it. If they're the slightest bit shifty, you can almost guarantee being convinced to pay an extra $10,000 to $60,000 more per property than the locals. The first step is to call your home phone company and get them to 'lock' or 'restrict' your number so it doesn't show up on the digital display of phones you call. That way, agents can't tell what kind of property prices you're accustomed to seeing, just by checking out your area code. So they are less likely to inflate prices, while still trying to make it sound like you could be onto a good deal.

Other things to watch:

- A message to your mobile phone by a shifty agent can sometimes give away which city you're in at the time the message is sent (depending on their phone features).
- Revealing that you're staying at a hotel, or catching a plane, or driving a rental car is usually a dead giveaway that you're not from that area and that you're probably working to a tight time-frame. These are green lights for slimy agents to try to sell you whatever they can, for whatever they can, as fast as possible—which is never a good recipe for success (sometimes even where reputable agents are concerned).

BUYING AN INVESTMENT PROPERTY THAT'S POSHER THAN YOUR OWN HOME

This option certainly sounds weird, but it can reap some unexpected rewards. For example, some posher and/or popular areas in Auckland and Wellington have leapt up to 70% in value over the last four years. So consider buying what you want to live in a few years from now, and rent it for five to seven years so tenants help you to pay it off. Renovate slowly while renting—or between tenants—and then move in once the taxman has helped you a long way towards debt-freedom. See your accountant for more details.

NOTE: People will always want to live close to work and city conveniences, and that by itself will drive prices of properties in towns surely—if reluctantly—upwards. But knowing this can help you use the greed of other people to your advantage, without actually being greedy yourself. (If that makes sense.)

PROPERTY BOOMS

Property booms can be as widespread as an entire city or as local as the top end of a single street, or they can even be focused into specific specialties, like heavy industrial land, office space, holiday units or houses with fifteen bedrooms, valet parking and swimming pools. So it would be fairly easy for an L-plate investor to crack a sweat trying to forecast or choose the best investment to start off with. But regardless of your situation, your boom property will usually outperform the others in its class, if it ranks highest on your checklist after investigating it thoroughly.

Spotting areas that will grow

Natural boundaries like creeks, rivers and hills often define the boundaries between areas that have vastly differing property values. In one area where I bought, vacant unimproved lots on one side of the creek were 23.8 times dearer than on the other—and you could physically jump across the gap when the creek was low. But the higher-priced blocks were presented neatly, as if belonging to an affluent area, while the lower-priced blocks had the look of a bad investment. They were overgrown. Their maintenance had been neglected, and their improvements were of poor quality.

Once we tidied up the place a bit and presented it as though it was loved, we didn't have to advertise to sell it. People went to great lengths to track us down and make offers. Just be sure that your 'rough diamond' has many or all of the attributes of the popular suburbs/districts nearby—like schools, shopping and easy access by car or public transport—and your place should boom.

NOTE: It's important that other owners/investors in your 'neglected area' are sprucing up their places as well, because a street full of nice homes attracts better tenants than one lonely nice home among rats' nests. So when shopping for property, keep your eye open for work being done in neighbouring homes.

Handy hint: Look for a nearby hill, lookout or tall public building where you can reach a high point to look out over a number of suburbs to help you spot natural boundaries between go-ahead areas and the ones that are lagging. In some places, you can practically 'see the money on the ground'.

As well as this, a bird's-eye view can help you understand what the problems may be. Sometimes a bridge over a river is all that's needed to improve access to the rough diamonds; or flood mitigation to prevent storm damage; or demolition of a central eyesore, like a row of derelict warehouses. Or there's another option that might sound absurdly extravagant, but if you can't get up high any other way, consider a chopper flight. It will cost you up to a grand, but it's tax deductible and could save you megabucks in the long run on your hundreds of thousands of dollars investment.

HOW MANY PROPERTIES SHOULD I LOOK AT?
As a rough guide, I like to look at about thirty properties, with inspections spread out over three or four weekends; and I usually prefer to look at no less than three properties in each area, so I'm comparing areas as well as value for money. Any less than thirty, and I think you're probably rushing your decision. Too many more than that, and you're probably just procrastinating—and annoying the shoes off your footsore partner.

HOW TO COPE WITH A BUSY OR BORED PARTNER
Go by yourself. Some agents don't like the idea of escorting only half of the decision-making partnership to property inspections, but they forget that many parents these days work day shifts while their partners work nights

so their kids always have a parent around. And not everyone can get a day off work at the drop of a hat.

Use the checklists from this chapter to put reluctant agents at ease for taking you out by yourself. Everything they show you will be documented thoroughly in the checklists and left on the kitchen bench for your partner to look at that night. At least half of the properties will be scratched off your list instantly as unsuitable, so you'll actually be saving time for your agents, not wasting it. You'll also be saving your own sanity if your partner is the type to complain every time they get sick of looking at other people's houses.

Anything that interests you will always get a second visit— and THAT'S the visit which requires ALL of the future owners to be present. So if agents offer to squish the first round of visits all into one day for your convenience, don't be tempted. Choosing a major investment takes time and if you can't spare it, then don't risk it.

Don't rush the process of house-hunting. You risk over-looking a problem that could cost you thousands to repair. At best, your investment will do far worse than it should have. At worst, it will become a lifetime liability as your dreams of wealth morph into nightmares of debt.

YOUR BLANK CHECKLISTS TO TAKE SHOPPING
Now that you know all about them, here they are, the checklists you've been waiting for.

Investment Property Checklist

> **YOU WILL NEED:** A clipboard with pen, binoculars, fridge magnet and a small loaded stapler, sunglasses and comfortable shoes.

Address:_____   Dates seen:_____

Most notable feature:_____

Price: $_____   Negotiable? Yes / No.

via real estate agent:_____ .   Contact Ph:_____

The Real 3 Ps:

The 1st P is for Position.
How close is it to:

	kms	Details and comments	Get there by score		
Schools:			**1**	**5**	**0**
a) **Childcare/kindy**			walk / bus / train / ferry / car?		
b) **Primary**			walk / bus / train / ferry / car?		
c) **Secondary**			walk / bus / train / ferry / car?		
d) **Uni /Polytechnic**			walk / bus / train / ferry / car?		
Grocery shops			walk / bus / train / ferry / car?		
Public transport			walk / bus / train / ferry / car?		
Arterial roads to/from city/industrial estates (=pollution / noise / tenant's jobs nearby?)			walk / bus / train / ferry / car?		
Hospitals/ambulance			walk / bus / train / ferry / car?		
Fast food/drive thrus			walk / bus / train / ferry / car?		
Parks/jogging or bike routes/other recreation?			walk / bus / train / ferry / car?		
Position score: (overall score out of ten)					

NOTE: All scores should be decided by YOU as it's potentially YOUR property that you're short-listing, but as a guide until your confidence grows, use walking distance as a full score; bus, train or ferry as half a score and car scores as zero.

Investment Property Checklist (cont.)

The 2nd P is for Popularity. Tick each detail as you go or use crosses if you're not happy with anything—so a tick = 1 point towards your popularity score out of ten. Note any comments from agents at the side to check later.

Tick	Detail	Comments
	Check capital growth for area over last year as per R/E agent's reports. (If it's down 50% on last year, that's dreadfully bad. If it's up 50%, that's amazingly good. Increases between 5% and 20% are more reasonable, but I wouldn't bet on jumps of 15% or more two years in a row without good reason, while 2% to 5% is often slow but steady.	
	Check for low maintenance: Cheapest homes to maintain long term are new lowset brick homes. Under 7 years, structure is still under warranty.	
	Standard of **street appeal** of other houses in the street. You're looking for a street or area where some houses have over-capitalised, so that when others catch up, the value of the whole area goes up. Or you're looking for areas where owners are already making big improvements. (Ex-government housing estates that have been cleaned up before selling don't usually count.)	
	How far away are industrial estates (km), military bases (km), large government offices or depots (km) or the city centre (km), so your tenants have a wide **potential job market** available?	
	Are any **shopping centres** approved for construction nearby? Shopping centres that are genuinely 'coming soon' means someone else has done extensive market research and ticked that suburb as popular for families with great growth potential.	
	Security: Is there a Neighbourhood Watch program or many other houses nearby with security systems to reduce risk of area being 'hit'? Is the area clean of graffiti /damaged street name signs? (Buckled street names = hoodlums roaming the street at night.) Also check street drains for discarded needles.	
	TV Reception: how many channels? ( ) Pay TV? Yes / no What's reception like? Any glitches?	
	Is the property **high enough out of the flood-plain** to have any view? If yes, it's more pleasant and less likely to flood. Drive up the largest nearby hill and look which way the nearest river/gully would flow when in flood. Beware of big, open drains pointing at the house.	
	Health & fitness: are there shady parks, paved walkways, bike tracks or gyms nearby? Every Kiwi from 0 to 100 loves to get outside, so homes with recreation facilities nearby feel attractive, even if they're never used.	
	Do any nearby main roads have tall **sound barrier fencing**? If not, but if it's nearby or coming soon, then quality of life will improve for tenants.	

Your score out of 10 for popularity:_____

The 3rd P is for Physical Traits. Each 'yes' tick = 1 point.
Each 'no' tick = possible bargaining chip.

OUTSIDE—Yard	YES	NO
Is there a non-leaky letterbox?		
Are all sheds, patios & extensions council approved?		
Is off-street and/or hail protected parking available?		
Is driveway paved to keep yard from churning up in rain?		
Is path from garage to house paved to keep mud out from tenants or kids who don't leave shoes at door?		
Do all downpipes look like they're connected legally? (A comparing glance over to neighbouring houses will do for now. Council regs for that area can be checked later.)		
Is the lawn free of damp spots which may mean busted pipes?		
Are power lines away from trees?		
Is the air outside the toilet wall and pipes odour-free? (If not, the septic is not working or pipes are busted.)		
Is the yard fenced well enough to keep dogs and toddlers in?		
If there's a pool is it properly fenced?		
If there's a greasetrap in the ground outside the kitchen window, is it easy to open for cleaning? (Or paved over? Double-check house plans later.)		
If there's a retaining wall, is it solid, rot-free, with no sign of erosion/sinking?		
If the house has a waste water recycling pit, does the pump still work? (If water stinks, ask vendors to add 'Actizyme' pellets, available from Mitre 10 or Placemakers, or buy it yourself and add it later to fix the problem.)		
Septic tanks; same as for waste water recycling pit above.		
If there's a steel flue or chimney, is the stack free of birdnests and rust?		
Is chimney straight, with rainhat fitted so rain can't come in like Santa?		
Stand back and look at roof screws/tiles (through binoculars if possible). Does all look well?		
Is ground outside toilet(s) free of big trees? (Roots may bust pipes)		
Total of Yes ticks out of 20:		

OUTSIDE—Walls & Roof	YES	NO
Is the roof bright & clean? (not aged)		
Are gutters free of rust, leaks and bad connections?		
Are gardens away from slab or kept short & tidy to protect slab warranty?		
Are gardens mulched to reduce weeds? (less work for you/tenants)		
Is the main power connection to house clean of burn marks and bare wires?		
Is the main power connection over one metre away from rainwater down-pipes? (If not, ask council or a power authority to check it, as the house may become live when gutters overflow.)		
Is inside of powerbox clear of spiders and burn marks? (TOUCH NOTHING INSIDE A POWERBOX!)		

The 3rd P is for Physical Traits (cont.)

OUTSIDE—Walls & Roof	YES	NO
Is the house fitted with a safety switch? (May also be labelled as Residual Current Device or Earth Leakage Circuit Breaker. Or it may be fitted to a special powerpoint or two *inside* the house.)		
If the house is on stumps, are all the stumps straight? (No spirit level is required. Your eye is usually good enough.)		
Do seals near windows look healthy? (Not flaky or cracked and leaky.)		
If your fridge magnet attracts to metal around windows/doors, is it properly rust-proofed or heavily painted?		
Is paint under eaves free of mould?		
Does paint under eaves look okay for another few years without repainting?		
Any obvious cracks in brick wall? (especially near window corners)		
Are signs of movement around slab or stumps less than 1 cms?		
Are downpipes colour co-ordinated? (White or clashing downpipes greatly reduce street appeal.)		
If there's a pool or spa, is the mortar in the nearby brick windowsills still firm? (If it's gone sandy the chemical spray has reacted with the lime and brickwork may need re-laying soon.)		
Total of *Yes* ticks out of 17:		

Before going inside use this space to jot notes of any 'no' ticks that you're willing to fix if the price is right:

_____

_____

_____

_____

_____

INSIDE—General	YES	NO
Do you get a good feeling when you walk in?		
Does the house smell fresh/clean?		
Are the rooms bright and airy?		
Are carpets in good condition? (Think of replacement timing and costs.)		
Is vinyl or lino free of pucking? (If sticky underfoot, it may need relaying.)		
Are any floor tiles broken? (If this house is shortlisted, come back later to check under all mats.)		
Is wall paint easy to clean? (If house is shortlisted, try a few spots later.) Are walls and ceiling paints in good condition?		
Are curtains/blinds in good condition?		

Your Investment Property Checklist (cont.)

Do wall and floor colours go with most styles of furniture? (If no, tenants often get frustrated after a while.)		
Are soft colours used on walls and floors? (Strong colours often stimulate strong moods in tenants.)		
Are security screens able to be opened easily in case of fire? (If fully fixed they may be death traps.)		
INSIDE—Wet Areas *(Loo, bathroom, laundry & kitchen)*		
Run taps in each room. Does hot water come through quickly?		
Do taps turn off quickly in blessed silence? (Or does water 'hammer' in the pipe?)		
Is the hot water system set at a safe temperature for kids? (If set too high, the system will boil constantly, costing money as well as water waste, both of which will make life inconvenient for tenants as well as dangerous.)		
Are the ceilings and walls in every room free of mould? (The roof may be leaking or ventilation may be bad, or incorrect paint may have been used in ceilings of wet areas like kitchen, laundry, bathroom etc.)		
INSIDE—Roof Cavity Is the ceiling access cover clean of fingerprints? (Ceiling access panels are usually painted to match the ceiling but ceiling paint retains marks easily Lots of fingerprints = possible trouble in the roof. NOTE: On your last, most serious inspection you may like to get your head up there to look around. Check for nail holes pretending to be skylights and rusty wiring or old insulation that will be a fire hazard.)		
Toilet Does the loo flush & refill properly?		
Has the cistern got a brick inside it to cut water usage? (If yes, check that chemical reactions haven't caused brass to turn green inside cistern.)		
Does the loo window still open?		
Is the skirting board firm and stain-free? (If yes, then loo probably hasn't leaked much.)		

Note: If any roof tiles, floor tiles, wall tiles, windows or permanent shower screens are cracked or broken, then make sure the vendor fixes them before or as a condition of the contract or else the valuation inspector may insist that you pay for the repairs BEFORE your loan can be approved. (The vendor may be able to claim them on his insurance or deduct repairs from the current tenant's bond.)

Total of *Yes* ticks out of 21 for inside: _____

+ Total of *Yes* ticks out of 20 for outside yard: _____

+ Total of *Yes* ticks out of 17 outside walls and roof: _____

= Total score out of 58 for Physical Attributes: _____

Then add up to 2 points if there's lots you can fix: _____

Plus total scores out of 10 for Position: _____

Plus total score out of 10 for Popularity: _____

=Total score for all pages out of 80 _____

Here's room for answers to extra questions

Postcode (needed to get a quote on average contents insurance, so you can tell if it's a high crime area):

Real property description (from rates notice—needed for departments and councils to answer your questions):

DP number:_____ Identifier :_____

Land Registration District:_____ Area :_____m²/ha

Current owners :_____

Is it currently rented?_____ if so: for how much/week? $_____

when is their agreement up for renewal?_____

would they prefer to stay on if possible?_____

Ask the owners (through the agent) if they've had any trouble with the tenants and to provide details of repairs or maintenance in the last 12 months: _____

_____

Ask the tenants (privately if possible) if they've had any problems with the landlord and if they want anything repaired so you can include it in the purchase costs: _____

_____

If this property will make it to your shortlist of top 3 choices, then also attach:
- a photocopy of the last rates notice
- a photocopy of the agent's map of the area (showing fencelines)
- a photocopy of the listing photo

(Ask for these things to be supplied by the agent, when you get back to their office.)

List of any equipment or furniture you want to stay with the house. (Never assume anything—such as plumbed-in-fridges, dishwashers or water pumps are included. To be safe, mention them as inclusions on the contract and make sure they're still there at handover.)

_____

_____

Other comments / questions you have

_____

_____

Notes to scoring *Your Investment Property* checklist

You should be able to tell straight from your checklist which properties deserve to be shortlisted. But these notes may also help you as a rough guide.

Scores under 30: Almost hopeless. If proximity is bad, its going to cost tenants time or $$ every time they want to do anything, so they'll expect up to 30% cheaper rent to compensate, and even if they do move in, they'll get grumpy and burned out travelling to work, or they may have their dole payments reduced for possible avoidance of the job market so they won't be able to pay your rent, even if they wanted to.

If it has less than 30% of desirable features or facilities, you're either looking in the wrong area or wrong price bracket if you want to attract good tenants any time you need them. So, scratch it unless it has a special feature like room to park a truck or room for kennels or a horse and you can fix its other problems cheaply yourself. (eg. city block that slopes down to river = riskier for floods, but room for grazing or jetty for canoeists.) Otherwise, it might be cheap to buy and a pretty enough or quiet enough suburb to live in yourself, but you'll have trouble getting and keeping tenants who need convenience and proximity to potential job market.

NOTE: If your agent shows you more than two of these, they're either not listening to you or they don't have much of what you want listed with their office. Ask what rental properties they've done valuation appraisals for recently, as many landlords ask for this before refinancing and may prefer to grab the opportunity of selling to you to increase their purchasing power somewhere else. (Some of the best deals are never advertised.)

Otherwise, ditch the agent and either try going through someone else or being your own agent (see also page 60–62).

Scores 31 to 59: Now you're on the right track. It has about half of the main commonly desirable features, but tenants are unlikely to stay more than a year, because they'll have their eyes open all the time for a better deal or will want to move if they get a better job. In the meantime, they're likely to complain about trivial maintenance problems which will seem more annoying because of their other inconveniences.

But it's worth paying attention to checking off every section on pages 3, 4 and 5 of the checklist for this one, if only for practice and so you don't regret crossing it off your shortlist later. Properties with scores over 50 will be worth a second look if you don't get many to choose from or can bargain a great price for it and fix most of its problems yourself.

Scores 60 to 70: A real contender. This one is going straight onto your shortlist. Make sure you've graded every section of the checklist and put a star on the bottom right-hand corner of each page, shifting it to the bottom of your pile (deepest under your clipboard clip) so you can find it easily when you get back to the agent's office. Then give your agent the list of details you need from the last page of the checklist so you can follow up on my favourite tips from chapters 8 and 11. Also use this property to compare with what other agents have advertised in their windows or newsletters.

Scores 71 and over for bargain-priced properties are usually too good to be true. Be suspicious. Be verrry suspicious. There could be a highway planned for the backyard or hatchet murderers living in the mansion next door. If not, consider renting it out only until you're ready to move in yourself . . . after all, having an investment home that's nicer than your own home is fine (and often very rewarding in more ways than just financially), but why should your tenants have all the fun once you're financially secure?

6

The Contracts

Signing a contract to buy an investment property can be even more involved than signing the contracts to buy your own house. There are the usual clause inclusions that go with the purchase of any property, but there's also the biggest decision you'll have to make: in whose name do you buy the place? The wrong decision can cost you thousands this financial year, as well as for every year you own the place plus one.

IN WHOSE NAME?

There are four options to consider: by yourself, as a joint tenant, as a tenant in common, or where a company you own plays the role of any of the first three. (Wherever a company is involved, you always need to seek the advice of your accountant.)

Did you know?

It's more and more common these days to see buyers putting the purchase contract in one name and writing 'and/or nominees' as part of their purchaser details to allow the final decision about whose name the property will be in to be made closer to the settlement date—which is fine when you're purchasing your own home, BUT . . .

If you don't know who in your relationship requires the most benefit from an investment property, or exactly how your purchase will impact on your finances, then what the heck are you doing signing on the dotted line for an investment property anyway?

How do you know that the best investment for you and your partner or company isn't in the Australian share market (see the Australian edition of *Your Money: Starting Out and Starting Over*. Or maybe your best investment is in New Zealand government bonds, or superannuation, or even debentures?

**Don't rush your investments!
Know what you're getting into and
prepare for the contracts *fully*
BEFORE you sign them.**

By yourself means that you're the only person who can claim tax deductions for your expense on the property. You're also the person who must add all income from the property to your personal income total before calculating how much tax you have to pay that year. You'll also have to make sure your Will stays updated at all times to ensure the property gets bequeathed, sold or managed according to your wishes after you've kicked the old bucket.

As a joint tenant means that two or more people own the property in partnership so both have to claim part of the income from it as theirs for tax purposes (usually 50:50 unless you have a very valid reason that's properly documented through your accountant). Both can claim deductions for expenses too. And if one dies, the entire asset automatically passes to the other person regardless of what it says in anybody's will. This is the method used in most husband/wife relationships, but if you would prefer your share of your house to go to your kids after you die so they always have a roof over their heads, then speak to your solicitor about using the next option.

As a tenant in common is very similar to a joint tenant situation, since income and deductions are treated the same way. But if one member of the partnership kicks the bucket, the family of the recently-deceased get to bicker over what happens to their new stake in the property or portfolio. With rising divorce rates and whole families starting to pitch in to buy one roof over all of their heads, this is the way that more and more contracts are being written, because—at any time you choose—you can make sure your kids, parents or other relatives from a previous marriage can still get a stake in your estate according to your Will, instead of having your share pass automatically to your property partner. As a tenant in common, you could also have an easier time claiming an unusual ownership split at tax time. For example a 60:40 ownership split between a highly paid partner and a lowly paid defacto would be better for tax purposes for both of them if they could honestly document how the higher paid earner made the 60% contribution towards ownership. See your accountant for more info BEFORE signing the contracts in case you can do even better.

As mentioned earlier, the choice you make here has major implications on your tax and income, not only for now but for as long as you

> ### Handy hint
> Having to speak to your accountant first before deciding whose name to put it in can also be a good excuse for putting off a pushy real estate agent, because you'd never sign a contract in one person's name, only to add another person's later—if you need thinking time, that is.

own the property. (Plus up to 12 months longer after you sell the place because you'll have to wait until the end of the final financial year for any adjustments to work its way out through your tax return.) So before finalising your decision on whose name to put on the contract, you need the following:

CRASH COURSE IN UNDERSTANDING TAX THRESHOLDS

The Inland Revenue organises income earners into separate wage brackets to make income tax easier on low income earners and tougher on higher earners. It sounds fair when you're a struggling individual tax payer, but include another ten to twenty grand for rent from ONE property a year and see what that does to your tax bracket!

For example:

- If you earn: $0–$38,000 per year, you pay 19.5% tax.
- Then for each dollar between $38,001 and $60,000, you pay 33% tax.
- Anything over $60,001 gets slugged with a whopping 39% tax.

Ugly to think of, but simple enough to calculate. You can see without needing a maths degree that someone who earns a total of $53,000 a year (from wages, rent from tenants and other income) will pay $12,360 in tax (forgetting tax deductions for the moment). That's calculated by working out each bracket one at a time so you get $7410 on the first $38,000 and $4950 on the extra income between $38,000 and $53,000.

> **Did you know?**
> One glance at the tax rates over $60,000 explains why so many people earning close to the upper brackets are turning down even higher paid stressful jobs or overtime in favour of more time with the family. The extra tax just doesn't make the extra effort worthwhile . . . unless you can legally avoid or minimise it—or even better, get it working for you, as I'll explain very soon.
>
> **Did you also know?**
> As a matter of interest, Aussies would pay over $16,000 in tax and medicare levies on the same income!

That's all there is to it, so . . .

If you have a family, with only one person working . . .
(and if you plan to pay out the place in three to five years so you can either keep it as a nice little income earner or sell it for a truckload of cash after renovating it or whatever), then put it into the name of the non-income earner. That means that this person won't get any benefit from negative gearing unless they take up a part-time job (because they don't earn a wage on which to pay tax). BUT they won't have to pay much—if any—tax out of the income from the tenant's rent either. And there's the bonus of paying far less on any clawback of depreciation when the place is sold.

For example, if the property was sold after two years for a capital gain of $70,000, then a non-income earning owner would pay tax on all the depreciation claimed on the investment building so far. It would become assessable income in the year of sale. In New Zealand, you used to be able to spread this 'clawback of depreciation' over three income years, but not any longer. (See also p. 108, Clawback.)

Also, someone earning $50,000 a year in rent ON TOP

of their normal wages would have to pay their standard tax on their income PLUS their standard tax on the rent from their tenants in whichever tax bracket that takes them up to PLUS the clawback of depreciation, which is probably going to be up in the highest tax bracket by then.

So it's obviously better for a lowly paid husband to pay tax on the depreciation clawed back so he can do it using the lower tax thresholds than it is to add it to a wife's $50,000 wage, which would mean the entire $70,000 would be taxed at the highest rate.

Summary table as a rough guide only

I could go into pages of examples here, but having read that first one, you should already be thinking along the right tracks. So following is a summary table of the most common situations with their most common solutions as

WHOSE NAME GOES ON THE CONTRACTS

	If you have a short-term ownership goal (under 8 years)	If you have a long-term ownership goal (8 years or more)
If both owners are fully employed and intend to stay employed	Buy in both names.	Buy in both names.
If only one of the owners is employed	Buy in the name of person who is going to be unemployed or lowly paid. They'll earn income from rent and have to pay tax on that, but any tax liability should be cancelled out nearly to zero by claiming the loan interest as a deductible expense. Then when you sell the property do it in a financial year (ideally) so your clawback of depreciation doesn't put you into a higher tax bracket.	Buy in the name of the person who is employed so that at least the interest is tax deductible. That person can then afford a long unpaid holiday in the financial year the property is eventually sold— minimising tax AND improving their lifestyle.

| If only one of you is employed now, but you intend to get back to work soon (1 to 2 years) | Buy in both names. | Buy in both names. |
| If one is employed and the other won't be returning to work for up to six years. | Buy in one name now and consider restructuring or selling and rebuying later. | Buy in both names. |

a rough guide to making it easier for you. Since income and expenses vary from person to person, always double-check these important decisions with your accountant.

If one of you intends to give up work in a few years to retire or raise a family, make sure you mention those goals to your accountant to ensure your decision is in harmony with your other investments, savings, superannuation, tax obligations and company dividends.

SPECIAL CLAUSES

It's important to remember that the standard contract you get through your local real estate agent or solicitor when purchasing or selling property is only the 'foundations' of your deal. Like any deal, you can add extras or delete provisions to suit yourself, so long as both parties eventually agree when it comes time for everybody to sign.

The draft contract you start with should bear the REINZ logo so you know that a widely knowledgeable panel of industry experts have all knocked heads over it at one time or another to make sure it's as fair to all parties as it can be.

You should ALWAYS take a contract away from a real estate agent's office UNSIGNED:

a) to avoid being rushed or bullied into a deal
b) to give your solicitor a chance to check all the possible extra clauses you can add, which may save your back-side for you if things go wrong.

Some of those 'this deal will only go through if' clauses include:

- subject to *your solicitor's* approval of results from the title searches
- subject to *your* approval of details revealed by the Land Information Memorandum (see page 61)

And my personal favourite—the one that saved me nearly two hundred thousand dollars in one deal:

- The subject to finance approval clause, as detailed below:

The 'finance to be provided by' clause

If there is a section in the contract for stating the specific bank, building society or credit union through which you'll be obtaining finance, make sure that it's filled in with the *specific* lender you've chosen to go through. Don't let the real estate agent put in a generic term like 'credit union' or 'financial institution' because your lender may find something wrong with the place and refuse finance for you—and you don't want the vendor or agent being able to force you to go to somewhere else for finance, if you don't wish to. However, most contracts do not state a specific lender, so requesting a 'subject to finance being approved by ABC credit union clause' to be added can be a very handy safety net for you, as a buyer, if the seller will agree to it.

BUYER'S REMORSE

Within three days of signing a contract to buy property, you'll often get sick to the stomach with worry. Everyone I know has gone through this stage. I still suffer the same feeling sometimes, even after all the successes I've had.

It's a fear of the unknown I think—that you've missed seeing a major problem with the place. Or perhaps it's a fear that you've just committed yourself to something that's going to take much longer than you'd planned to pay off. Or sometimes it's because you see a property that you might have liked better, for a much lower price, as soon as you've committed yourself elsewhere. But that's okay.

Opportunity is everywhere—it's just that you never noticed it until your eyes were open. So if you see other opportunities as soon as you've signed a contract I think that's actually a reassuring sign that there'll always be something worth looking at whenever you're ready to buy again. But if you think you really *did* rush your decision, just accept it as a heavy payment for a hard lesson (especially if you've bought property in a state where you're not covered by a cooling off period. Contact your solicitor or the Real Estate Institute for more details.)

As for those other fears: well, I've found the best way to combat them—especially for those first three days after signing a contract—or at least until you get the results of all your property searches—is to look back over your property checklists and reassure yourself that you made the best decision based on the best opportunities and best information that was available at the time.

Did you know?

I once signed a contract on a lovely three-bedroom brick home, but my bank discovered a rather large underground mine shaft just below the surface and told me that if the house didn't fall into its own cellar within a decade, I'd be lucky. So they pulled finance out from under me and I actually celebrated having my loan application rejected.

With some fancy footwork from my solicitor, a lot of support from the ladies at my building society and the clause that bound me to getting finance specifically from them, my bacon was saved.

(See? Banks may have a bad rep for their conditions, but they still have some great people behind the counters!)

7

Your Choices for Tax, Tax and More Tax

Be warned that whenever you buy a large income earning investment, you can discover a whole new world of hurt when it comes to tax. The good news is that just when you've come to resent the truckloads of cash that bolt from your paypacket every pay, becoming an investor entitles you to a whole new world of tax deductions, concessions and rebates that for too long were the secret back door to wealth for people who were already earning indecently generous incomes every year.

We've got a bit to get through here, so I'll try to stick to the biggest tricks and traps that I've found. (Just remember that I don't have any formal qualifications—only personal experience, either from my own purchases, or from my experience in helping friends and others.) Let's start with the biggest curse to any wage-earner—tax that slugs you straight from your paypacket.

PAYPACKET TAX (also known as Pay As You Earn, or PAYE) Imagine what your paypacket would be like if you never had to pay tax again. That's the best case scenario of course—and there's always strings attached. But it's definitely possible, by using one of the best pieces of paper

---

Handy hint

Some of the hints that follow may be used by ANY wage-earner who makes a lot of donations or gets paid a lot of allowances for either phone or car or tools etc.—even if they're not trying to negative gear any kind of investment. So even if you don't decide to go ahead with your first investment property purchase right now, you may still be able to use the info in this chapter about Form IR 23 BS to make your tax life easier in the short term.

---

to come out of the Inland Revenue Department: Form IR 23 BS. (Second only to a fat cheque for a tax refund.)

NOTE: The full title for this little gem is 'IR 23 BS—special tax code/student loan special reduction rate application'. Somebody hand me a Panadol! Imagine reading this section if I didn't abbreviate it!

FORM IR 23 BS—THE MOST FUN YOU'LL EVER HAVE WITH THE IRD

Form IR 23 BS allows you to apply for the unthinkable: the right to get back giant chunks of the tax you pay—not as a lump sum at the end of the financial year as you might normally expect, but in easy-to-manage slabs with every single paypacket! I call them 'mini tax-refunds' every pay.

In real terms, a Form IR 23 BS is an application form which asks Inland Revenue to give you a letter to send to your main employer authorising them to take less tax out of your paypacket every pay for the rest of the financial year (or sometimes for shorter periods). You can't write your own letter to ask your pay officer to do this because your employer will get roasted by the taxman for failing to fulfil their obligations under complicated tax laws. It takes the official IRD authorisation to let them do it.

> Just imagine your paypacket without any tax deducted!

Now imagine the money that you used to pay in tax being used to pay off an investment property (or your own home, or a shares portfolio).

Combined with the income from your investment—whether it's hay grown off a vacant block or rent from tenants in a house, industrial shed or shopping centre—you may not have to make up any of the standard repayment out of your own pocket at all! (That's the trick AND the trap behind most of the property investment schemes and scams that are out there today, but more on that later).

> **Warning:** Every mini tax-refund you get through your pay is that much less that you'll get in your tax refund at the end of the year.

The size of the deduction depends on the size of your loan, as well as your deductions and income for the year. As far as tax from your paypacket is concerned, even if you don't get it reduced to zero, making this application can still shovel wads of semi-reliable extra cash into your wallet every single pay to help you get ahead faster.

Of course, you could blow your mini tax-refunds at the casino, pub or cinema every pay, or on repayments on a flashier car or annual holidays overseas, but that's not going to get you what you really want—fast financial security. For that, in my experience at least, you need this money to pay off your personal home loan or investment properties.

> **Handy hint**
> Use the tips on page 134 *Income from all directions* to set up repayments with this tax money, so it's fast, fun and easy to take care of.

Don't be daunted when you see Form IR 23 BS
It may look like it's written in typical government red-tape gobbledegook—and in some places it is—but this document is much easier to cope with than it first appears. Here's how.

You will need
- A Form IR 23 BS (or two of them, if your spouse is part owner of the rental property or negatively geared investment and wants to get some of their tax back every pay too).
- A blue or black ink biro.
- Your most recent payslip.
- Your employer's details.
- Income forecasts of all your income for the current financial year, including wages, dividends, interest, rent from tenants, and income or losses from businesses/ partnerships/farms. (*Handy hint:* To avoid a tax bill at the end of the year, or to avoid delays or problems getting next year's Form IR 23 BS approved, it's best to slightly OVER-estimate your income.)
- Forecasts of your deductions for the current financial year, including work-related expenses, donations, tax losses from previous financial years and expenses for maintaining or buying your investment property or other investments. (*Handy hint:* To avoid a tax bill at the end of the year, or to avoid delays or problems getting next year's Form IR 23 BS approved, it's best to slightly UNDER-estimate your deductions.)
- You'll probably need a vat of coffee too—and about half a packet of Tim Tams.

Where do you get it?
You can ask for a hardcopy of Form IR 23 BS to be posted to you by phoning the Inland Revenue helpline on INFO express (forms and stationery line) 0800 257 773. You

need to have your IRD number handy. Or you can print a copy straight from their IRD website at www.ird.govt.nz and when that screen loads, by entering the keyword IR23BS into their searchbox.

(See also *handy hints* and *nasty traps* on page 105–106.)

Did you know?

- **There are no limits** to how small an amount you can request to be 'refunded' regularly with this form. But you may consider the effort in paperwork to be more than it's worth if you're only going to get up to $15 less tax out of every paypacket. It's a matter of choice—or desperation—for that extra cash.

- **You can be legally cheeky** and get reduced tax taken out of your pay using Form IR 23 BS, even if you don't have a loan for an investment property. Do this by claiming 'tax reductions' for your regular paypacket for things like investments in the film industry; large or regular donations; motor vehicle, travel; phone or tool allowances which are paid to you by your employer; or for any other income-related expenses (so long as it is approved by the Inland Revenue). It's worth looking into because, for example, if you get motor vehicle allowances of around $10,000 or more a year, then imagine using 100% of that towards fuel, maintenance or car loan repayments, instead of losing up to 39% of it in tax until you claim it back at the end of the financial year. Ask your accountant or the Inland Revenue for more details.

- **IR 23 BS can also be used to INCREASE the tax from your paypacket**, but spare cash is always best kept 'parked' in your high cost loans (eg. over-

drafts and mortgage offset accounts) to save you big bucks in loan interest until just before the deadline to pay any annual tax to the IRD.
- **The IRD puts out a great info brochure for small property investors in the form of IR 264**, which can be posted to you by calling their Info Expressline on 0800 257 773, or can be downloaded from their IRD website for free at: www.ird.govt.nz/library/publications/geninfo/ir264.pdf

A bunch of handy hints before you start
- Requesting the form by phone will mean it takes up to a fortnight to reach you even if it's in stock, while printing a copy off the website costs you about eight minutes of internet time (if you've got a slow rural connection, like me) plus travel to your local library or internet cafe, if you don't have internet access at home.
- Approval only lasts until 31 March each financial year, so you have to reapply each time. Get ahead of other investors and avoid defaults on your automatic repayments by timing your renewal Form IR 23 BS to arrive at the Inland Revenue as soon as possible BEFORE 1 April each year.
- Approval letters are sent directly to you to sign and then send to your employer. To avoid delays with your pay office, I suggest you hand it to your payroll officer immediately and with a friendly smile, so they can let you know right away how soon they'll be able to drop the amount of tax you're paying.
- Don't start any automatic loan repayments which are funded by your mini tax-refunds until you get your first paypacket with them working properly, or you could be slugged with default fees by your bank (if there's not enough in there already to cover the first repayment).

Nasty trap: Your application will only be processed if you've supplied your pay office with your tax file number using a tax declaration form AND if you've lodged ALL required tax returns for previous years AND if you don't owe the Inland Revenue Department any money (including any tax debts from last year). So get cracking on all those shoeboxes full of receipts and scribble out a cheque to get your tax debts up to date. (Or see page 107 for hints on how to get rid of a tax debt quickly.)

Do it now!

Delays in submitting the form costs you delays in making extra repayments, which are far more expensive than you may realise. For example, if you're at the beginning of a $100,000 loan over 30 years or more (at 8% interest) then every extra $10 repayment you make now translates into a whopping $98 that you DON'T have to pay over the full term!

More handy hints for using IR 23 BS:

- Form IR 23 BS is a breeze for the most part, but if you have any questions about it AFTER reading the instructions and having a fair crack at it yourself, ring the Inland Revenue Department Info Expressline on 0800 257 773. (You'll need to have your IRD number handy—and remember BE FRIENDLY!)
- To play on the safe side, don't forget to OVER-estimate your forecast income a little, and to UNDER-estimate your forecast deductions to avoid a tax bill at the end of the financial year AND to avoid rejection or delays to approval of your next year's renewal form (called Form IR 23 ES).
- Your new tax rate will only be applicable for the periods shown on the Special Tax Code Certificate that will be sent to you (called IR 23).
- Your renewal form (IR 23 ES) will be sent to you automatically in time for next year, but if your circumstances

change in the meantime, you'll have to notify the IRD immediately (and return their approval certificate within 7 days if requested to do so) or you'll risk making them grumpy—and we don't want *that* to happen, now do we?

Handyhint: To play on the safe side, don't forget to OVER-estimate your forecast income a little, and to UNDER-estimate your forecast deductions to avoid a tax bill at the end of the financial year and to avoid rejection or delays to approval of your next year's form IR 23 ES (which is your renewal form).

Warning: Every tiny detail can be double-checked and thoroughly verified by the Inland Revenue so to avoid delays and audit problems, double-check everything first BEFORE you send in your application form.

HANDY HINTS TO GET RID OF A TAX DEBT QUICKLY

In order to reduce the amount of tax taken out of your paypacket, you usually have to pay out any tax debts you have before the Inland Revenue will process your Form IR 23 BS application.

If it will take only a few months to pay off a tax debt using income from your paypacket, then try to do this first, or else consider deferring the date from which your mini tax-refunds will apply, so that the money still goes to the Inland Revenue on your payday but is now 'effectively' used to pay off your existing debt in the meantime. (See Q11 on IR 23 BS for more info.)

Other options include:

a) Decrease your 'extra' deposit (any amount over 20% deposit, which you had hoped to use in reducing your loan) enough to pay out your tax debt at the time you take out your loan to buy your investment property. Costs: Loan fees on the extra loan PLUS interest rate usually 6% to 9% and paid off over the full term of your loan PLUS any extra deposit needed to avoid paying mortgage indemnity insurance on the loan (if you were already borrowing close to 80% of the property value).

b) Take out a cash advance on your credit card—interest rate usually 12%–19%—paid out over whatever period you choose. *Handy hint:* Then 'park' your grocery, fuel and bill-savings in your credit card until you need them—withdrawing them without cash advance—to keep the interest bill down as much as possible before you have to spend the 'parked' money.

c) Take out a personal loan or overdraft—interest rate anywhere between 9% and 35%, plus establishment fees. NOTE: Only suggested as a last resort where tax benefits will far outweigh your expenses.

Reminder
For details on how to understand your current tax thresholds, see page 94.

DEPRECIATION, CLAWBACK AND POOLING
Now that you'll be earning thousands a year in rent from property, you're entitled to claim depreciation (an ageing allowance) as a tax deduction for anything which suffers wear and tear in the process of earning that income for you. Since everything ages differently, the Inland Revenue provides volumes of specific guidelines for anything that can be claimed, but the most common depreciation guidelines you'll need to know are:

Buildings, construction costs and improvements. You can get a yearly tax deduction for your building's original construction costs, renovations and new fences, sheds or other capital improvements over $2000. And improvements under $2000 can be 'pooled' together and depreciated using the average value of the 'pool'. The trap/trick with this being that the IRD publishes a list of recommended rates of depreciation for each type of item that is allowed to be depreciated (samples below), and that you'll have to depreciate your 'average value of your pool' by the depreciation rate that belongs to the lowest rate for an asset in the pool. Sounds complicated, but it's not really. You can segregate an asset out of the pool at almost any time when you notice when it's the financially best time to 'retire an item off' to personal use and replace it with a newer brand/model to depreciate within the pool (and therefore raise the average value of the pool again).

Generally speaking you can use either a straight line method (SLM)—or a diminishing value method (DVM) to calculate your depreciation of your capital costs, where rates vary depending on what year you built, purchased and/or renovated the building. And if your building was constructed or purchased before the end of the 1995 income year, depreciation may also depend on if it has a wooden frame or not.

Buildings purchased or built during or after the 1996 income year must be depreciated by either:

a) 4% of the previous year's depreciated value using the DVM; or

b) 3% of the initial purchase costs every year (year in, year out) if you're using the SLM.

Buildings bought or built between 31 March 1993 and 1995 can either use the above methods for depreciation, OR . . .

a) buildings with a wooden frame can be depreciated using 3% by diminishing value method or 2.5% by straight line method, whereas . . .

b) buildings with concrete, brick, stone or other frames can be depreciated using 2.5% by diminishing value method, or 2% by straight line method.

Definition Alert!
The two methods of depreciation are easiest to explain by example:
If you bought $2200 worth of carpets for your investment property last year, then using rates from the table on p. 111 you could either depreciate them.
a) by the Straight Line Method where:
$2200 x 28.8% = $633.60 every year for about 3.5 years.

Or...
b) by the Diminishing Value Method:
Year 1: $2200   x 39.6% = $871.20
Year 2: $1328.80 x 39.6% = $526.20
Year 3: $802.60 x 39.6% = $317.80
Year 4: $484.80 x 39.6% = $192.00 . . . etc.

For more information, see IRD Booklet IR260, called Depreciation.

NOTE: Investors use the DVM when they need the biggest deductions in the first few years of ownership (often because they're using principal and interest loans, where interest costs are biggest at the beginning too. The DVM is also best suited to investors who plan faster ownership and/or a short term sale). Whereas the SLM is mainly used when you need more consistent levels of tax deductions over the full term of ownership. You can mix and match your financial structures for each property differently however, so always discuss your long-term goals with your accountant when you're planning which way to go.

Fixtures, electrical appliances and other depreciable items. These wear out faster than the building, so they depreciate faster. Examples at current rates of depreciation (purchased after 1996) include:

SAMPLE ITEM	%DEP USING DVM	%DEP USING SLM
Curtains, fridges, freezers & ovens	26.4	18.6
Carpets, TVs, videos & stereos	39.6	28.8
Dishwashers, washing machines & dryers	31.2	21.6
Lawnmowers	48	36
Loose furniture, light fittings & vinyl floorings	21.6	15

For more information, see the back of Inland Revenue Form IR3R, and also their booklets called *Smart Business* (IR320) and *Depreciation* (IR260), which are all available from their website www.ird.govt.nz or by phoning them on 0800 257 773. You can also call 0800 377 774 to discuss your specific questions about depreciation directly with the IRD.

NOTE #1: There's a handy online depreciation rate finder at: www.ird.govt.nz/cgi-bin/form.cgi?form=depnrates which also links to a great depreciation calculator at: www.ird.govt.nz/cgi-bin/form.cgi?form=depncalc

Other interesting info about depreciation in New Zealand:
- Depreciation is calculated on the number of months in a year that the item was used or available for use to produce income, but you can't claim depreciation for any asset in the year you sell it, unless it's a building.
- Most repairs and maintenance (for cars, computers, etc.) can be written off as business expenses in the year they're incurred, instead of depreciating them.
- Assets costing under $200 each can usually be written off in the year they're purchased.

- Profits and/or losses from sale or disposal of buildings and other depreciable items are treated as income and/ losses in the year the item is sold or scrapped.

Clawback
When you buy a building as an investment property, you claim depreciation for it in your tax return every year (as I've just explained). Ideally, the government grants this so you'll be able to afford to repair or replace the building when it's old and run down. (Most people don't plan their future that way however, usually spending the tax refunds instead, when they should be saving them for when the time comes.)

Each year the building and other depreciable assets are worth less and less 'on paper', regardless of how well you're looking after the place to keep its value. Which means that most buildings are sold long before they rot into the ground and—hopefully—for more than what you paid for them.

This means Inland Revenue will want some of their money back. From their point of view, they only 'loaned' it to you as depreciation adjustments until you sold or disposed of the place and could work it out exactly. The sad part, from our point of view, is that Inland Revenue wants to claw it back off us in the year we make the profit, which is usually when we've already set our hearts on buying that new Roadster we've been drooling over.

There are things you can do to reduce the 'depth of the claws' on your wallet however:
1. Clawback is taxed according to your top tax rate in the income tax year in which you sold the property, so plan ahead by selling it in a year when you can either:
   - take a 'paper loss' in the stockmarket or elsewhere to offset your profit
   - take a few months off work as an unpaid holiday to study/have a baby/raise young children/ recouperate from an illness or injury

- retire or reduce your annual earnings in any other way

. . . so the clawback portion isn't taxed so much in the highest tax bracket.

2. You can also reduce the effect of the clawback by being able to prove that most of the profit stems from an increase in the land value, rather than an increase in the value of the building (and other depreciable items sold with it). You can do this in a few ways too:
   - You could hire a reputable valuer and hope their report agrees with you.
   - Your first and last rates notices can prove how much the unimproved value has risen (or fallen) since you bought the place.
   - Your purchaser's first rates notice (if valuations rise soon after you've sold) can show how much the council recognises that the sale of your property contributed to their need to increase unimproved land values (upon which they levy their rates). NOTE: Unimproved land value info can usually be obtained from the council at any time by post for a small fee. But if you're friendly and make it a quick phonecall, they may even tell you for free.
   - Before and after photos of the yard can show how you've converted a disgustingly overgrown, weed-ridden and uneven block into a tidy or even prizewinning showpiece of lawn or garden by sweating over your own garden shovel. Your own labour is not usually depreciable (unless you're invoicing one of your own companies for 'their' services), which means your undepreciated labour was worth all your blisters and sweating after all!

Handy hint: As anything wears out (close to $0 value on

paper) replace them with new ones to start depreciating again while the old (but not completely useless yet) ones can be disposed of back home or at the tip.

Beware: If you sell any item for more than its depreciated value (worked out to the exact day you sell it) you'll technically be making a profit which you'll have to pay tax on. So instead of selling your old, depreciated items from investment properties (eg. old lawnmowers, not-quite-dead air-conditioners and worn carpets) at a profit, consider selling them at the current depreciated value, or 'retiring them off' to your personal use, or donating them to charity (preferably getting a valuation and tax deductible receipt in the process if you can).

Items written off: Some items can be written off in the year you purchased them, which is the same as saying that their depreciation rate for the year was 100%. Such items include: rates, mortgage insurance and building insurance, repairs which do not add value to the property, and mortgage interest (provided it's only the portion which is not split for use for your own home loan, car, or to pay off other debts). Legal fees to arrange the mortgage are also deductible, even though the legal fees in buying and selling the property are not. Cleaning and gardening costs are okay, however. So are home office expenses like internet connection and stationery. Motor vehicle expenses are also permitted (the portion of your car that's not used as personal expense, of course). And finally, real estate agent fees to collect the rent and manage the property for you—if paid by you—are also fully deductible.

Things you CAN'T claim as tax deductions against your rent income include:

- Private expenses or the private percentage of things you use to earn income with your investment property (eg. a lawnmower or high-pressure water pump, which you use at home, but also use in mowing your lawn and washing down your exterior walls).

- The percentage of the year that YOU lived in the property.
- The percentage of the year the property wasn't available for tenants. (Being vacant is okay, so long as you would—and could—have put tenants in, if there'd been any wanting to go in.)
- Capital expenses which increase the value of the property.
- The original purchase price of the property.
- Interest on the portion of the loan which you use for reasons OTHER THAN purchasing the property (even if you use the property as security for the entire loan).
- Real estate agent and legal fees in buying or selling the property. (These have to be capitalised and depreciated. See your accountant for more info.)
- Accounting fees—you CAN claim a deduction for paying an accountant to prepare your accounts, but you CAN'T claim any of their fees for setting up a business or researching the investment viability for you beforehand.

GST AND YOUR INVESTMENT PROPERTY

You can't charge GST on the rent that your tenants pay you, because rent is exempt from the GST legislation. This also means you can't make a claim in a GST return for any expenses you incur while trying to earn rent from your investment property. But you CAN claim the GST portion of your expenses as a tax deduction when you're claiming your deductions against rental income. NOTE: Property developers who buy investment properties, or investment properties which earn income other than rent, may have to pay and collect GST. (Contact your accountant or local Inland Revenue office for more info.)

8

My Favourite Tricks Before Settlement

You've signed the contracts. Finance has been approved. There's nothing to do now except wait . . . or is there? The limbo period between signing the contract and settlement is often unbearable. For most people buying their first investment properties, the clock couldn't tick any slower. But if you want to get financially ahead of the pack, this time should be your busiest.

YOUR BUSIEST TIME

1. Start making repayments as soon as the loan is approved. It doesn't have to be standard repayments, any amount will do, as long as it's as much as you can afford during this time.

   How? By asking your bank what the loan account number will be—and regardless of whether the person behind the counter says you're allowed to or not, try making account transfers into your loan account as soon as the loan has been approved. The worst that can happen is that the transfer gets rejected and the money stays in your savings account.

   NOTE: Loan approval means that the loan account has been set up on the bank's computer so it will be just sitting there, waiting for settlement date to tick past. The bank will be using it to deposit your application monies, withdraw their fees and enter the starting amount of your loan so that your first statement is a full record of every transaction relating to the property— but no interest will be charged to you during this period. So if you can make any extra deposits or repayments during this time, you'll be reducing the 'effective' starting principal of your loan, which does two things:

- It makes the standard repayments instantly a little more than they ever really need to be (because the standard minimum repayment calculated by the bank was worked out for the planned balance owing, not the reduced balance owing).
- And it ensures that you never pay any interest on the portion of the principal that you repay before settlement.

And yes, it IS perfectly safe to make repayments on a loan before the property is legally yours—yes, even if the deal falls through—because the loan account is YOUR account. Any funds left in it after any fees are taken out simply get transferred back to YOUR savings account.

2. Also get ahead by getting access to the property to clean it up, renovate it or prepare it for making income from day one of your ownership. Yes, if the deal falls through and the property doesn't become yours you will be giving away anything you spend on the place (unless you include some kind of renovation clause in the contract). But you shouldn't be doing anything to the property until you're 100% sure that the loan has been signed, sealed and approved.

3. Widen or clear the easiest access to and from the largest door in the house so that large furniture can be moved in easily without damaging gardens, paths, walls or doors, wherever possible. Remember, good tenants want their furniture undamaged and the walls unscratched too, so make it easy for them to keep both of you happy.

4. Fill in your Form IR 23 BS and post it to the Inland Revenue as soon as the loan is approved, with a note attached to the front advising the settlement date and asking them to authorise reduced tax from your first pay date after settlement. Yes, the settlement date is provided inside the form anyway, but bringing it to the Inland Revenue's attention on the front and asking them (nicely) for their prompt attention may prevent your application going into someone's 'don't have to approve it yet' basket.

5. Create a 'house file' for your own records—a large ring binder with clear plastic page inserts will do. (See page 122 *Creating a house file* for details.)

Handy hint

If a loan falls through for any reason, ask your bank how long you have to buy another property without having to pay full loan application fees again. One building society I used would not refund the valuation fee I paid because the valuation had already been done before the deal fell through. But they did offer to hold the application open for 12 months, allowing me to put the address of the new property onto the loan application later that year without having to pay anything more than a second lot of valuation fees—which I also escaped because the rates notice showed that after my large deposit was paid, I was borrowing less than the unimproved value of the land, Pretty cheeky, huh?

6. Create a 'welcome sheet' for your tenants so they know how to work everything, find everything, and have details of how to contact you, your property manager and emergency services if ever they need them. (See page 124 *Creating a welcome sheet* for details.)

> **The longer the contract period, the more things you can do and the more money you can save.**

Handy hints: I always try to buy properties on a three-month contract instead of the more common four to six weeks between signature and settlement. Real estate agents won't like the idea much because they have to wait until settlement to get paid their bonus/commission, so they may try to talk you into a shorter arrangement. But vendors often agree because it gives them more time to organise moving house.

So if your real estate agent or vendor tries to talk you into a shorter settlement period, try saying you need the longer time to finish saving up for your deposit, so you'll have it by settlement. For a double-income couple, a three-month settlement gives you between 12 and 14 extra fortnightly paypackets to play with before settlement.

7. Be respectful of your vendor's personal privacy. Don't show up every second day to drool over your new purchase—no matter how tempting it may be. Discrete drive-bys are okay, but until they move out, make viewing appointments about once every three to four weeks so you can check up on any measurements or colours for renovations (and save time and lawsuits later by making sure they're not stripping the place of anything that was included in the contract).

8. Ask your tenants what day the property will be vacant so you can have a large 'Beware of dog' sign hung on the front gate as soon as they leave. (Even if you don't have the dog, a kennel and chain with the chain leading out of sight of anyone looking in from the street will deter the neighbourhood light-fingered-Larry.

9. Remove the 'sold' sign from the front gate as soon as you can. The real estate agent owns the sign, so you can't throw it away until they fail to collect it when asked—and they won't be in a hurry to collect it, because a sign with a 'sold' sticker on it is good free advertising for their company. Unfortunately, it's also a neon indicator to thieves of an opportunity to break in.

QUIZ QUESTIONS TO ASK BEFORE SETTLEMENT

Now that you've signed the contracts and the vendor doesn't have to 'gloss over' anything to convince you to buy the place, do yourself and your future tenants a favour by quizzing the current owners with the following questions to save time, money and hassles later.

*   Are there any water usage restrictions?
*   What day is garbage collected?
*   Is standard and recycled rubbish supposed to be put into separate bins?
*   Is there a building covenant for the area? (ie. minimum standard of prettiness)
*   How many dogs (or cats) are allowed by council? (Some councils will accept registrations of pets from other councils, so tenants don't have to renew their pet licences until the new year.)
*   What is the soil type for gardening purposes? (eg. neutral, alkaline or acidic? Different plants have different needs and you could spend big bucks on plants that all cark it within a month if they don't like the soil.)

- Does the owner still have a record of the soil type for building or renovating purposes? (eg. is it stable, reactive or highly reactive?) If the current owners can't tell you, ask them to retrieve the information from their building plans or from council before settlement because some councils charge a fee, which they may choose not to charge to the person who paid them application fees in the first place.

- If there's a pool or spa, ask the vendors to ensure the chemical balance is correct on handover day and that water levels are full in the pool and/or spa before water meters are read. (Meters are usually read on the day of, or the day before settlement, unless other arrangements are negotiated.)

- If town or rural water is to be turned off by council, ensure all toilet bowls and cisterns are full beforehand, as you may need to flush before it's reconnected. Reconnection usually costs under $100, but is better out of their pocket than yours, if you can negotiate it.)

- Ask current owners for copies of invoices of all items still under warranty. Structural house warranty is usually seven years, but warranties on vertical blinds, awnings, floor tiles, carpets, vinyl, glass windows, shower screens, steel roofing, spas and steel sheds may all have current warranties if they're under ten years old. Also, any items like waste water recycling pumps, hot water systems or ovens may have new individual warranties that you need to know about. Why pay for fixing or replacing something in a year or two if you are entitled to it free of charge? (If invoices aren't available, ask for details of the companies who supplied the item/s, what month the goods were supplied and the name of the company or person who paid the account. Request photocopies of the relevant receipts or invoices from the suppliers now, before you need them.)

- Ask current owners or tenants if they can please leave behind any colour samples or building surplus that may have been left over from when the place was built, so you can use them for any renovations, or to take shopping with you when trying to colour match other new decor.
- If there's a grazing paddock attached, I ask current owners to remove their animals as soon as possible before settlement to let the grass grow back, but still keep the perimeter slashed/mowed neatly as a fire break. That way the property is attractive to tenants as well as to their animals.
- Ask current owners to teach you how to handle any temperamental equipment like roller doors, security systems or pilot lights for hot water systems or gas ovens—and take notes. Type them out neatly for your tenants and add them to your 'welcome sheet'.
- Ring the companies that provide your car insurance or home and contents insurance and ask if changing the garaging address of your car or shifting of your current contents to your investment property would cause your premium to go up, down or stay the same. Their answer can often give you a good indication of the crime rate in the area where your tenants will live compared to where you're living now.

CREATING A 'HOUSE FILE'

Save yourself time and hassle down the track by putting together a 'house file' now, while you have the opportunity. (A house file is just a record of what the house looks like, inside and out. You can have it as a section in your property management folder (see Chapter 11), but my house file is usually a large apple box, because samples of floor coverings, roof sheeting and floor tiles are usually all too bulky to file in any folder.

> ### NOTE
> Wise tenants and landlords will take a photograph of any damage that already exists in a rented house or business premises—getting the other party or a Justice of the Peace to sign the back of the photo to confirm that it was like that before tenants moved in. Signed conditions reports are a poor substitute for a picture, no matter how wordy the description is.

A house file should usually contain:

- Colour photographs of each room exactly as they would appear to tenants on the day they move in (be they furnished, semi-furnished or empty). Cut the dated headline off a local newspaper to include in close-ups of existing damage and also in clean undamaged rooms, so you can prove later if any extra damage was done by new tenants. NOTE: Settlement day is the best day to do this, but extra snaps before the current people move out can save you dollars too. If you're paying for a $400,000 home and a football-sized hole gets knocked in the wall while the current tenant is moving out their wardrobes, you can show that the damage wasn't there when you set your price, so it can become the current owner's responsibility to fix before settlement, instead of yours. (Sometimes you may need to stick up for yourself like this, because excesses on insurance premiums might make it pointless to lodge a claim.)
- To help with any future renovations or repairs, you might also include any colour samples of carpet, curtains, wall paint, tiles, or vinyls that you can find left in any cupboards.
- House plans and other property-related documentation lodged with the council.

- A photocopy of the street map for the local area so the taxman or your accountant can get their bearings easily during an audit. (It also looks impressive in your file.)
- Keep an eye out for business cards of tradesmen who service that area and stick them onto a page in your file for future reference.

CREATING A 'WELCOME SHEET'

Most tenants will be moving in from another area and will appreciate a 'welcome sheet' which lists local attractions, supermarkets, fast food outlets and instructions for the oven, gas heater, hot water system, roller doors and security system etc.

Much like the folder of information that you find in any hotel room, the welcome sheet might sound like a lot of work, but if you do it up as a laminated 'menu' or brochure, nailing it by a string to the inside of your pantry or linen cupboard, then you'll only have to do it once for all future tenants.

If you get really keen—especially if you have a PC with MS Publisher or some other creative document program—you can reproduce your 'welcome sheet' as a 'brochure', perhaps even including a scanned photo-

---

Did you know?

One young thief caught during a break-and-enter in my area had a photocopy of a lands department map folded carefully in his back pocket. Larger than a street map, it had details of fencelines, lot numbers, street names and major buildings.

'What are these red dots for?' asked my police friend while arresting him.

'Houses with dogs,' replied the thief, rubbing his bitten backside. 'Only I missed this one.'

graph or two of the house to advertise it for rent on community noticeboards. Leave a few on the kitchen bench under a paperweight on viewing days, so prospective tenants can take one as they look through. They're much less likely to forget your property or get details about it mixed up with others they've seen that day if they have something semi-professional to take away with them.

I'd also recommend including the contact name, work and after-hours contact numbers for your property manager on your 'welcome sheet' in case there's an emergency (burst waterpipes for instance). And I'd also include details of a mobile phone number or post office box number so they can contact you directly, if they fail to get satisfaction from the property manager.

If you're managing the property yourself, then I'd also include the bank account details for (preferably automatic) transfer of the rent money; and a list of tradespeople for your tenants to contact to get emergency repairs IF you or your property manager are unavailable at the time. Of course, you should specify a limit—perhaps up to $300—to both the tenants and the tradespeople beforehand. That's usually enough for small emergency repairs. If it's something that's insured, you could write a sentence permitting them to start getting three quotes for repairs (eg. in the event of storm damage or the like, so that any inconvenience to them or extra damage to your property is kept to a minimum).

Finally, don't forget a welcoming slogan, perhaps something like:

'Welcome to our second home. Like you, we're just trying to survive financially until our retirement and we hope this lovely home will help us along. Please treat it well, and we shall ensure that it always keeps you in comfort.'

Or maybe:

'Welcome to our second home. Please act welcome to remain welcome.

Thank You.'

9

Paying For It

Okay, so you've chosen the place, got the right loan and now it's yours—to pay off. You'll have income coming at you from at least three sources—from your job, your tenants and your tax returns. And while expenses attack you from all directions, you'll have massive repayments to cope with as well. So here's how.

HOW MUCH WILL REPAYMENTS COST?
You can manipulate the size of your loan and its repayments by bargaining down the purchase price or manipulating the size of your deposit. You can also manipulate the property income you get by negotiating the rent levels you charge. And you can manipulate the size of your tax benefits by:

- Making capital improvements so you can depreciate them over a number of years.
- Timing what financial year some repairs are made so they can be written off in the financial year that you earn the higher income (and therefore need more deductions to keep your tax low).
- Pre-paying interest for the next financial year (but only

if you have an interest-only loan and need a big tax deduction this year).

- Choosing to make extra repayments which drops the interest you pay for the year. NOTE: Extra repayments also drop your tax deduction in proportion to the lower interest.

But regardless of the assortment of manipulations you use to manage your overall investment debt, there are three main approaches you can take to paying out investment or business loans—and it's wisest to choose early because you can't shoot for a goal unless you know where the goal-posts are. So decide between the following, depending on how strict you want to be with yourself. (The stricter you are, the faster your capital grows.)

Option 1: Not very strict. Make the full repayments straight from your paypacket and then use your tax benefits and the income from the property to pay your living expenses (and buying anything else you want, such as holidays, cars or more investments). Advantages are that you can guarantee repayments even if the property is vacant or not earning income for any period. Disadvantages are that it's easier to over-indulge in lifestyle expenses during the good times, and impossible to survive at all, let alone stress-free, during the bad times.

Definition Alert!

'Strict' does NOT automatically mean hard on your lifestyle.

Strict—for any mortgage or financial strategy—means carefully planned and executed. Any compromise you CHOOSE to make in lifestyle in the SHORT TERM is nearly always compensated for exponentially—both immediately AND in the long term.

Option 2: Stricter to set up, but easier to live with. Aim for a loan repayment that's roughly equal to the rent you get from the property so your tenants are paying off the loan and then your tax benefits can be used towards property maintenance, improved lifestyle and/or your next investment. Advantages are that somebody else is paying off your loan. Disadvantages are that you need a larger deposit, a reserve fund to make repayments in case the house is empty for up to a few months, and the ability to increase rent or fund part of the repayments from your own paypacket if interest rates skyrocket. (Yes, option 2 is usually the one that's marketed by all kinds of property advisors under all kinds of guises to make ownership of your first investment property feel easier, cheaper or even free.)

Option 3: Strict to very strict. Any combination of the above that suits you. For example, to pay out my first three investment properties in only one and a half to three years each, I put a stranglehold on my budget and paid as much as I could afford from my/our pitiful paypackets—which was usually about a full repayment by itself anyway. PLUS, I used all of the nett income from the property. PLUS, I used up to 50% of tax refunds on repayments as well. (NOTE: The rest of my tax refunds went towards maintenance and capital improvements. That way, the property value AND effective capital was increasing much faster than by inflation alone.)

Even so, accountants all over the country are turning white after reading how fast I paid off my investment loans. Many will argue that I should have used interest-only loans or paid out the principal over the longest possible time to maximise the number of years that I get the largest tax benefits by staying in debt. But I would argue that I owned three properties completely debt-free by the time I was 25 years old and then had every cent of my income to invest or spend any way I chose. I only ever got back a portion of my loan and other expenses through tax benefits anyway, so continuing to pay out the rest of my pay or profits for as long as the loan existed would have been 'slow financial torture' for me. Fast ownership started out as a personal choice—partly because I couldn't stand the thought of a lifetime in debt and partly because banks can change the terms of our loans without our permission, and I didn't trust them to keep my loan affordable over the next 30 years. But as a bonus, fast ownership bought me fast financial freedom.

HANDY HINT FOR REPAYMENTS

I like to take out 20 to 30-year loans, so the minimum repayment is the lowest possible in case I get struck by hard times. But *I choose* the effective length of the loan by increasing the repayments to whatever I can afford without compromising the lifestyle I want at the time. So that makes repayments *always* higher than standard monthly repayments set by the bank. Fast ownership—even of my investment properties—helped me get where I am so quickly. It's safe, flexible, reliable and practically guaranteed to give you a giant leap ahead because every single buck you pay off your loan is instantly converted into capital—which means you haven't spent it at all, you've just converted it into something else. On top of that, your extra dollar in repayments now will mean up to ten bucks in repayments, interest and fees that you don't have to make over the term of your much longer loan.

> **Some people call this positive gearing.
> I call it determination and common sense.**

HOW MUCH FROM YOUR POCKET?

Here's a few rules-of-thumb to help you with forecasts before you buy. They're only a guide and may not apply to every situation, but they help give you some point from which to start your calculations, even before you go house hunting.

Rough rule-of-thumb for rent: Because of the way many landlords borrow money over the long term, rent is often charged at between 5% and 10% of the property value to cover costs. So if a property is worth $250,000, you'll often see rent charged between $12,500 and $25,000 per year. (That's about $240 to $480 per week.) Obviously, less popular properties charge less to attract tenants, while better homes in convenient or popular suburbs sometimes get away with charging more.

Rough rule-of-thumb for expenses: I like to budget 3% to 5% of the property value per year in maintenance and running expenses which is a little higher than most landlords. However, budgeting it doesn't necessarily mean you have to spend it all every year. Stingy landlords might scrimp on repairs and pocket the leftovers as profits. Cautious landlords might hold the leftovers in a term deposit, high-yielding savings account, or mortgage offset account, so they're more prepared for problems in future. And keen landlords might churn the unspent portion of their annual maintenance budget into capital improvements to increase tax deductions and potential rent as well as increase capital so they can borrow against it to buy more homes.

I prefer a combination of these—shopping around for the best quotes when making repairs; buying carefully without scrimping; as well as keeping a portion for next year's reserve for repairs AND spending some on capital improvements—which also serves as a reward to good tenants, by the way. (Improvements in a rental home are like saying 'look after the place for me and every six months or so I'll improve it for you with something nice, like air-conditioning or automatic roller-doors for the garage, or a security system, or fly-screens or whatever.) You can also park your maintenance budget in your mortgage offset account—if you don't have one set up specifically for that purpose—to keep loan interest down so your own home loan drops faster.

(Very) rough rule-of-thumb for annual tax

Step 1: Work out how much tax you pay every year from your paypacket and write your answer here:

Partner 1:_____   Partner 2: _____

Step 2: Work out how much rent you expect to get a year from the property and subtract the amount you expect to pay in loan interest, bank charges, maintenance and repairs. Write that amount here: _____

(If it's positive, it's a profit. If negative it's a loss.)

Step 3: Work out how much tax you would pay on the amount from Step 2 by using the tax brackets on page 94. (eg. If your annual income is say $35,000 from your employer, and your rent income is say $10,000, then the first $3000 of your rent income would be taxed at 19.5% and the rest of it, in this case, $7000, will be taxed at $33%. If you make a loss above, then deduct that from your gross paypacket income and work out how much tax you should have paid and the difference will be a very rough approximation of how big your annual refund is likely to be, without considering any other factors. NOTE: If you're buying the property in joint names, then split the rent income (minus expenses) in half before calculating how much tax you have to pay. (Or use whatever other percentage extent to which you are partners or 'tenants-in-common' or 'joint tenants' on the title to the property, eg. 40:60 or 20:80. Most husband and wife purchases are assumed by the Inland Revenue to be half and half. If you want any other percentage you will have to be able to justify it. Speak to your accountant for more details.) Tax refund/debt:

Partner 1: _____   Partner 2: _____

Rough rule-of-thumb for working out your repayment contribution

Step 1: Write your standard weekly loan repayment here: $_____ (or use $1/4$ of your monthly amount.)

Step 2: Work out how much rent per week you will get (less 3% for maintenance): $ _____

Step 3: If you expect an annual tax refund from the previous rule of thumb, divide it by 52 to work out how much tax you hope to get back every week using Form IR 23 BS: $_____

Step 1 – step 2 – step 3 = the minimum amount that you have to contribute. (If this amount is negative, you may have overclaimed your mini tax refunds on Form IR 23 BS (or ES).

MORE ON MANIPULATING YOUR DEBT-MANAGEMENT

I mentioned earlier that as an alternative to paying off your investment property quickly, you can set it up to be on the size of loan YOU choose by lawfully manipulating certain aspects of it, like the deposit and purchase price, until the property virtually supports itself from its own income. Here are some of those points again—with a few more—explained in greater detail:

Manipulating the loans: As you've seen already, you can manipulate the amount you need to borrow by increasing the amount you have available for a deposit or by negotiating better loan costs or a lower purchase price before you sign anything.

Manipulating the repayments: The repayment requested by the bank is only the minimum required to repay your loan. You can increase the repayment by any amount you can afford—aim for double but even $5 a week is worthwhile. You can't decrease it to below the minimum monthly repayment, however, without falling behind and incurring hefty fees or having to refinance.

Manipulating the property income: Just because the going rent for a house in your area is $240 a week, doesn't mean you have to charge that if the extra amount is going to throw your taxable income into the next tax bracket. This is where the reduction of a few dollars in rent can be worth more in getting or keeping good tenants. So don't be afraid to DROP your rent a little if it is better for your particular financial circumstances.

Manipulating the tax benefits: As the end of the financial year draws to a close, do a quick tally of your expenses for the year. If you think your taxable income needs to come down a bit to put you into a lower tax bracket, talk to your accountant about undertaking extra expenses that suit you. Or maybe your finances could benefit by repairing something on your investment house—even if your tenants haven't complained about it yet. Or you could build something new on your investment home—like a small pergola, a new internal fence or a garden shed, to either depreciate individually or charge the average value of your 'pooled' assets. (See also page 108 Depreciation Clawback and Pooling).

INCOME FROM ALL DIRECTIONS—SET AND FORGET

If you're a good money manager, go ahead and lump any tax you get back into one giant repayment with other contributions towards regular repayments. One transfer out of your savings account to your loan account looks tidier on a monthly statement. But if you're less confident (or someone who likes to see your statement dropping by little chunks more often) then I recommend setting up separate automatic repayment authorities with your bank—one for each source of money for your repayment.

That's probably going to be:

- one from your nett paypacket—whatever you wish to afford
- one that equals the rent you charge (minus a small amount that you put aside for repairs and maintenance)
- one that equals the amount you get back in tax through your paypacket
- and maybe one for each and every other source that you may like to devote to repayments—for example, any regular electronic payments, pensions, second employer or regular pocketmoney from your great Aunt Winifred.

Doing it this way helps slip your financial goals into auto-success mode. It also makes budgeting easier, because you can practically set and forget everything you handle this way, leaving the rest of your income budget for your personal enjoyment. It also means you won't spend anything here by accident. And you can adjust or cancel one or another easily without affecting the others.

Yes, your statement has heaps more transactions on it, but it shouldn't cost you anything in extra bank fees, because in most cases the money can be deposited directly by the person who's paying it to you. (And because you should have already made sure you are using an account that offers unlimited—or a high number of—free internal electronic transfers every month.)

Arranging each small repayment independently also gives you the satisfaction of seeing how every little bit helps. And if one transfer gets missed because of funds getting delayed, it doesn't stuff up your entire repayment for that period which could put you behind, as well as slug you with default fees.

10

Managing the Place

From toxic tenants and miserable managers to bonds, interviews and dubious developers, this chapter aims to fill you in on some of the most important day-to-day management tips you'll need once you have that first investment property of your very own.

TENANT TURNOVER

Four sets of tenants in seven months is horrendous to think about, but it happens—and with alarming regularity, particularly with rental properties aimed at people with middle to lower incomes.

Whether tenants are moving in or moving out, it's only natural for floors, walls, door jambs and paved or concreted driveways to get knocked around by the increased traffic of furniture moving in and out.

Half the problem, I strongly suspect, is NOT the tenants. Sure, work transfers and marriage breakups account for a good portion of the mass-furniture-migration problem. But it's also interesting to note that real estate property managers sometimes word their management agreements so that—in addition to their weekly commission (see page 140 for details) they also get to keep the equivalent of the first one or two week's worth of rent as payment for the extra work they have to do to find and interview new tenants. So the more often they turn over tenants, the greater their own income. However, this situation may change if the proposed legislation is passed.

That's not to say that every property manager is out to rip you off like this—because it's not easily done—but theoretically, you can understand how the ones with borderline reputations get tempted. Put simply, in any areas where the number of rental properties available for management is basically static—and that's practically every suburb where vacant land is a rarity—property managers don't usually have any trouble 'finding' tenants. The area is already fundamentally popular if it's completely full of houses. So 'finding' tenants is a lot easier in many cases than the fee involved might indicate. You only have to ring some agencies to let them know that you're looking for a place to rent, and they'll take your name and number and add you to the bottom of their long waiting list. Only the reputable firms check references and invite you in for a thorough interview.

Property managers also feel pressured to maximise profits from the properties on their books when other real estate agencies or property managers pop up in their area like weeds. With only a fixed number of properties available for rent and more managers for owners to choose from, there are less profits for the original agencies. Therefore, higher tenant turnovers become one of the few ways to compensate.

But managers can't just kick out tenants whenever they feel like it. Strict guidelines in modern rental agreements give tenants the security they need (and in most cases deserve).

The trap for landlords and tenants alike is when property managers—either deliberately or through neglect or incompetence—fail to attend to the tenants' complaints about maintenance needs for the property. Nothing annoys tenants more than if they have to complain a dozen times about a hot water system that can't heat water enough to turn a baby's toes pink. At the same time, nothing annoys owners more than if they've instructed the manager to get quotes for repairs and the managers either muck you around for weeks with quotes that are over-inflated, or get the work done by handymen who charge you like a roaring bull but give freebies to the managers who send them regular work.

It's true that there are some stingy landlords out there, but in my experience, the majority of owners these days know that keeping well-maintained properties means keeping good-paying tenants, not to mention higher capital growth. So I think the legend of lousy landlords is perpetuated to some degree by lazy or slimy managers.

Handy hints for bypassing this problem

Tenants can bypass the problem by asking the property manager for the owner's contact address in order to directly report problems that remain unfixed. (They'll either get satisfaction faster, or they'll figure out who the real problem is.)

Contact addresses for actual landowners can also be obtained (either free or for a small fee) from the relevant local authority, or sometimes from the rental bond authority.

Owners can bypass this problem if they:

- Provide tenants with your contact phone number for emergencies (preferably just a mobile number so they can text message you when the phone's turned off and can't harass you at home later if they turn toxic). Consider giving them a post box address too so they can put their concerns to you in writing if your property manager fails to fulfil their obligations.

- Try to negotiate penalty clauses for managers if tenants are forced to complain directly to owners, or if owners have to take over organising the repairs or quotes, or when you can show that you've been overcharged consistently by quotes arranged by the manager.

NOTE: Some of this section paints property managers out to be the bad guys when very often it's the opposite. I've always preferred to use a real estate agent as a manager whenever I can, because I'd rather be horse-riding or painting or swimming than chasing other people for money. But managers have nearly cost me wads from my wallet at times too, by requesting replacement of expensive fixtures when all they needed was a little tweak. (Like a hot water system that was boiling dry—not because it was stuffed—but because it was turned up too high. And a house pump that was pulsing tank water loudly through the pipes in spurts—not because it was desperate for a plumber—but because the tank was cavitating and needed a little more air, using a bike pump.)

MANAGEMENT FEES AND/OR COMMISSION ('let fees')
If you hire/contract a real estate agent or dedicated property manager to manage your property, you'll have to pay them a commission—also known as a 'let fee' which is often in the vicinity of 8–8.5% of the rental income per week plus GST, and variation from that usually depends on what services they provide to tenants, including condition reports, bond lodgements, tenancy agreements etc. There will be an additional fee—often the equivalent of the first week or two of rent—for finding, interviewing and selecting tenants for you, if you wish.

Beware: When you purchase an investment unit or apartment in a building where all the dwellings become available for rent at the same time, many landlords in the bigger complexes will find themselves competing against each other to secure their tenants first. Real estate agents, large-scale investors or other property managers may even write to you, encouraging you to hold out 'allegedly with them' so you can all enjoy achieving tenants who pay the highest dollar rents possible. A fine idea, but too often their ulterior motives can be questionable—perhaps either to keep their commissions at the highest rates possible (which can benefit you too), or so they can slip tenants into or their own or clients' dwellings behind your back, while your property stays vacant waiting for the top rents. Prepare to be bullied. Or better yet, avoid the situation as best as possible by looking for tenants as soon as you know the settlement date or building completion date.

RENTAL BONDS
Rental bonds are not compulsory, but they are a wise precaution—a bit like an insurance policy—where you may request tenants to pay a bond—usually worth between two and four weeks worth of rent—from which you can deduct money if tenants cause accidental or deliberate damage that needs to be repaired. However, bonds can also be used to claim against unpaid rent, removal of property left behind, or cleaning if the house is left dirty or overgrown.

Ask for your bond before the tenants move in, preferably giving them your bank account details so the money can be transferred to you electronically—with no delays for you and no fees for them. (Or a property manager will handle all of this for you.) Note: You can also ask for up to two weeks' rent paid in advance.

The bond is your main security against tenants breaching the terms of your tenancy agreement. Although not compulsory to ask for a bond, there are strict rules and limits for them if you do.

For example, the bond is NOT for spending on the house. It has to be kept safely and refunded to tenants in full when they move out without any problems—or in part if you need to pay for repairs out of it. The Tenancy Services Centre operates a custodial service where landlords must send their rental bonds for safe-keeping within 23 working days of receipt and failure to do so may result in some fairly nasty penalties. (If there's a bank guarantee involved as the security, then different conditions may apply to lodgement of that too.)

You can only charge one bond for each tenancy agreement however, and additional bonds for items such as keys or for keeping pets are a strict no-no. You're also breaking the rules if you try to charge a bond to help cover the costs of complying with your obligations to the Residential Tenancies Act or the Tenancy Services Centre in your province.

Receipts for bonds paid to you must be signed by you and show the following details clearly:

- your full name, as the person receiving the bond
- the name/s of the tenant/s who paid it to you
- the date they paid it to you
- how much it was (including how much was put up by each tenant)
- the address of the rental premises
- the physical address for the landlord and the tenant (not a post office box).

> Bonds can also be requested if you're renting out your own home while you're away on holidays.

Then you both have to fill out a joint landlord and tenant agreement—often called a lessor/agent and tenant agreement. And you have to sign a bond lodgement form which you have to send promptly to the Tenancy Services Centre.

NOTE: The paperwork for lodgement of the bond should only mention the people who paid the bond—which may not necessarily be the same names that you put on the tenancy agreement. For example, the tenancy agreement may be put in the names of a single dad who's moving in with a tribe of little kids under his wing, while the bond may be paid by the non-custodial mother who lodged it as part of an out-of-court settlement after their marriage broke up.

As a matter of courtesy, you can make sure your tenants have a copy if they don't get one directly from the Tenancy Services Centre.

Bond loan program

Under certain circumstances, Work and Income New Zealand will provide loans to tenants for rental bonds (called Accommodation Supplements and/or Tenure Protection Allowances) if they're low income earners and if the weekly rent is within a certain range and if the property provides a certain basic standard of living. As a landlord this won't affect you much, except that it helps to know if your tenants are struggling to repay their bond loan, as well as making rental payments to you every week. (Contact Work and Income for more details. Ph: 0800 559 009 or www.winz.govt.nz)

Partly paid bonds

You can allow your tenants to pay their bond by instalment if they don't have the bond you want. It's a lot of extra hassle and paperwork, but it can help you get the tenants you prefer, if they don't have the size of bond you want before they move in. In such cases, the first bond instalment will usually be lodged on the standard bond lodgement form within the required time-frame, while subsequent instalments are sent in as soon as you get them (sometimes on a special instalment lodgement form).

Refunds, claims and disputes

Since you're dealing with a government authority, there are separate forms for refunds, claims and disputes. If all parties agree, the bond can be retrieved by supplying the Tenancy Services Centre with a claim form that's been signed by all parties. Tenants can have their portions of the bond refund returned to them by direct credit to their bank account. Or, by getting your signature on a Bond Transfer Form, alongside the signature of their new landlord, they can have their bond refunds forwarded to their new landlord.

NOTE: If you had to give your tenants a 'notice to leave' form, or if they've given you a 'notice of intention to leave' form, then the application to get your bond monies back can't usually be paid until after they've moved out and given the keys back to you.

If there's a dispute over who should claim part or all of the bond, then any of the parties can make a claim for the bond by lodging the specific form—even if the tenancy agreement hasn't terminated yet—so long as the tenants have moved out. The Tenancy Services Centre alerts all parties involved that there is a dispute and if you can't come to an agreement then you can use yet another government application form to request the Tenancy Tribunal to make a decision for a small application fee. (See also p. 234 for other helpful organisations and their contact details.)

Warning: No bond—or portion of the bond—will be paid to anyone until the dispute is resolved.

DIY TENANT INTERVIEWS

A property manager often conducts the selection process for tenants for your property as part of their service. Good managers will interview tenants thoroughly, run credit checks, verify personal references and check master databases of tenants who have a history of turning toxic. So in choosing to do it yourself and opting to select your own tenants, you'll have to do all of these chores yourself AND cope with the toxic tenants who have been blacklisted by the professional managers and don't have anywhere else to go.

You'll also experience the joys of bargaining with the cunning end of the tenant gene-pool who realise that by managing the property yourself, you're trying to save the management commission plus any fee that you'd pay to the manager for processing costs each time they have to find new tenants for you.

In a suburb where there are plenty of vacant properties waiting for tenants, there will be an unenjoyable amount of room for negotiation. But if housing is in short supply, the bargaining chips will be back on your side of the table. But either way, if you're going to conduct your own tenant interviews, you'll need to be prepared for the kind of questions they're going to ask.

Your first questions from tenants

Usually these come via a phonecall. Someone has seen your ad and wants to know more. There's no need to give exact street addresses yet, since there's no fun in advertising to potential thieves when the house will be available to rob. But you could leave a list of these questions with answers

---

Handy hint: Save time and repetition during the interview by preparing an info pack for your tenants to read before the interview begins. Include a brochure on the property, its features and details, plus an information sheet on the main terms and conditions of living under your investment roof. That way you won't have to dwell on depressing things when you're talking to them in the interview. You can just refer to them and explain them further if required.

beside the phone so others in your family can help callers who might otherwise find lodgings with another landlord before you can get back to them. They'll want to know:

- Which suburb is the property in?
- How many bedrooms has it got?
- What are its main features?
- What is its security like?
- What car accommodation is there?
- What is the weekly rent?
- Is it currently occupied?
- How soon will I be able to move in?
- Has it got a fenced yard?
- Am I allowed to keep pets?
- Am I allowed to advertise for housemates?
- What day is the rent due?
- Will you be collecting rent in person, or can I deposit directly into a bank account?

Your first questions for tenants should include
- What's your name?
- Do you work, and if so, where?
- What suburb are you living in now?
- Why are you leaving?
- What rent are you paying now?
- Have you got any children, and if so, how many and what ages?
- Do your kids go to kindergarten, daycare, school or university?
- What pets do you have?
- What breeds are your pets?
- Are they vaccinated, registered with local council and in good health?
- Have there been any complaints about your pet(s) with previous neighbours?

- Do you mind if I contact your current landlord to check references?
- Have you had any problems with your old landlord, and if so, how did you resolve them?
- What is your landlord's contact phone number?
- What is your contact phone number?
- When is the best time to call?
- Do you have a waterbed?
- Do you have contents insurance?
- Have you ever had the phone or power disconnected? If so, why and for how long?

For cat people
- How many cats do you have?
- Have they been spayed or neutered?
- Do your cats use a litter box?
- Do you allow your cat(s) outside?

For puppy lovers
- Has your dog been spayed or neutered?
- Does your dog need a big yard?
- Have you and your dog been to obedience classes?
- Do you need to keep your dog chained up for long?
- Does your dog bark, howl, snap or is it likely to attack if I call to collect the rent?
- Do you usually allow your dog inside your home?
- How does your dog get along with other dogs and people?

For fishy folk
- How big are your fish tanks?
- Do you mind keeping them off carpet areas?

Later, at the interview, tenants will want to know
- How long a grace period can I get if I go through a rough patch and have trouble scraping together rent?

- Do you offer a lease arrangement? (How long is it?)
- Would you have any special conditions for renewing the lease later?
- If my housing needs change, do you have any other units/houses etc. available in other areas where I can move to?
- Can I advertise for people to share (if not already discussed)?
- Can I sublet?
- What utilities am I responsible for?
- And they may also wish to know if they can contact previous tenants to see what kind of landlord you are.

At the interview, you should clearly outline
- What penalties you have for late rent payment or for breaking the lease.
- What utilities you expect them to pay.
- What maintenance, cleaning or gardening you expect of them for the rent amount you're asking.
- How often you need to conduct inspections (respecting their privacy of course, and making appointments or setting times which will be convenient for them too).
- What your limits and expectations are on keeping pets, hosting parties and allowing friends to sleep over.
- How you or the council expect garbage to be disposed of.
- What security measures the house has installed.
- Any codes of conduct for the housing estate or building complex as a whole.
- Your limitations on customers coming to a home office.
- What modifications they have to notify you of before commencing (eg. wall papering, shelf installation etc.)
- Whether or not you would consider selling them the home on a rent–buy basis later on.

You should also check at the interview if they're neatly presented and not loud or obnoxious by nature.

TENANCY AGREEMENTS

Tenancy agreements between the landlord and the tenant must be in writing, but do not in any way over-ride the rights and entitlements of either party under the law. For instance, a tenancy agreement may say that the landlord only has to give the tenant a day's notice to move out, but the Residential Tenancies Act (1986) states that tenants must be given either 42 days notice or 90 (depending on circumstances), so the manual clause in the agreement becomes useless. It's therefore important that all parties fully understand their rights and obligations (available from your local Tenancy Centre—or see head office contact details on page 235) BEFORE attempting to sign anything.

Blank tenancy agreements and inspection reports (which should be filled out by both landlords and tenants at the same time) are available from all Whitcoulls retail outlets for $1.95 each, or in 5-packs from the New Zealand Property Investment Foundation for $5, or they can be downloaded for free off the Housing Ministry's website: www.minhousing.govt.nz/tenancy/Forms/tenancy%20 agreement.html

Important points to remember about the tenancy agreement include:
a) post office boxes cannot be provided as addresses on any part of the form
b) the landlord must give a copy of the agreement to the tenant BEFORE they move in
c) no blank sections should be left on the form
d) if a bond is paid, a Bond Lodgement form has to be processed as well
e) all bonds have to be lodged with the Tenancy Services Centre within 23 working days of being paid

f) both tenants and landlords must respect each other's privacy under the Privacy Act 1993

g) the tenant may (currently) have to pay a fee for any services provided by any solicitor, real estate agent or property manager relating to the granting of the tenancy

NOTE: Tenancy Agreements also have great info on the bottom about your rights as a tenant or a landlord.

BIGGEST SNAGS TO DIY
The biggest snags in doing the landlord thing yourself lie in your isolation from industry networks that can protect you.

For tenancy history checks to see if your prospective tenants have ever defaulted on their tenant agreements before, property managers at real estate agents and other large-scale professional property managers can get security access to an online database managed by the Tenants Information Centre Australia, generated by data from TICA's 12,000 members and inclusive of records for New Zealand now too. The only way private landlords and even most investor clubs can check prospective tenants against the TICA database is indirectly, by employing a real estate agent to select your tenants for you.

However, some property owners' associations are working towards replicating a network database like this, so keep in contact with the landlord support group in your province for the latest update.

For police history checks, some large-scale property managers will ask tenants to complete an authority to allow checks to be conducted. Of course, any Police Department processing fees are passed on to the landlord through the managers' fee. Private landlords can try asking prospective tenants to supply a police history certificate, just as a very security conscious employer might. (But certificates are necessarily vague on details to protect privacy, and usually only happily supplied by someone who has nothing to hide, making them not terribly useful to most private landlords.) However, a police certificate might reveal if someone has a long history of drink driving offences or unpaid parking fines—which could be a symptom of someone who has trouble paying rent—but you have to be careful not to discriminate against a prospective tenant for unrelated ancient history.

Credit history checks are sometimes done by professional property managers too, but this is public information that's available for a fee. Private landlords can pay for bankruptcy and/or credit history checks by contacting a business research company or debt collection agency.

The snag with credit checks is that you still have to be careful about discrimination in using information to choose one tenant over another. Also, these management costs can mount quickly without providing any tangible guarantees that tenants are either toxic or terrific. In the meantime, you can get a rough idea of how someone handles their money by asking if they have a mobile phone that's on monthly or quarterly account or if phone companies will only let them have one that's prepaid in advance. Interviewees might also confess if they've ever had the power or phone disconnected. And owning up to having two or more credit cards, uninsured furniture and an unroadworthy or unregistered vehicle are all usually bad signs as well.

Toxic tenant insurance is often provided for property investor network members against default on rent payment or deliberate damage for only those properties which were bought through their club/network, while some property managers can provide this service for any properties they manage. But the private landlord can often get this too through a national insurance broker by simply checking your local *Yellow Pages*. Sample premiums include: $273 per year for a $120,000 house, $436 per year for a $200,000 house and homes valued over $300,000 by individual quote. Suburb and security features may also affect premiums.

Toxic tenant insurance

Not quite as hard to get as pet insurance, policy names can vary from company to company. So ring a broker to ask about insurance against toxic tenants defaulting on rent or causing malicious damage and you might get a giggle, but at least they'll know right away what you're looking for.

Property condition reports are organised by reputable property managers before and/or after tenants move in or out so that claims against the rental bond for damage repairs can be processed. The snag for private landlords is that you'll have to do all of that yourself, involving inspections, thorough record-keeping and lots of paperwork to fill in for the rental bond authority. (Fun for people who get passionate about managing their own properties, but a pain in the backside for everyone else.) Don't overlook the use of an instamatic camera or, for the more expert of landlords, a video recording of the property to enable you to record its state before tenants move in and after they move out.

INTERVIEW YOUR PROPERTY MANAGER, RENTAL AGENT AND/OR INVESTMENT ADVISOR

If the idea of chasing rent money and conducting regular inspections doesn't turn you on much, then paying a property manager either yourself or through a property investment scheme can be a time and sanity-saving expense that's also tax deductible. But just because they manage lots of properties, doesn't make them good at it. Use Appendix III again to compare managers carefully. Then:

- Ask each of them for the contact numbers of three ten-ants and three landlords for whom they currently work so you can check that everyone's happy.
- Compare charges for finding your tenants as well as ongoing management commissions (let fees).
- Ask how often inspections are conducted and how much notice you need to provide in order to go with them sometimes.
- Ask if you can still do some of the management duties for a discount. (Or if you're going through a property investment network/club/scheme where you're doing some of the management duties anyway, ask if they'll help match you with another landlord in your area so you can be witnesses for each other whenever things get a bit hairy.)
- Ask how tough they are on property presentation, providing examples of some of the things they've picked up on in the past and how they've managed to get the tenants to fix the problems.
- Ask how many properties they currently manage and how much personal experience that particular person has on the job. (Sometimes tiny teenaged receptionists manage more properties than they could reasonably handle.)
- Ask if they have security access for tenancy history checks with TICA. (Maybe they've been kicked off. Ask for evidence or try ringing TICA in Australia on 612 9743 1800 to check.)
- Ask if they do police record checks and credit history checks, and if so how. (The fibbers probably won't know.)

- If the property manager is a slightly built person—as is often the case—ask how they cope with large aggressive tenants.
- Also ask how long their vacancy waiting list is.
- And finally, ask what their average vacancy rate is.

NOTE: Try asking these last two questions BEFORE you buy the place, firstly as a potential landlord wondering if the agent would be willing to manage the place as well after you've bought. Then have your partner or friend ring back (later) wondering the same thing from the point of view of a prospective tenant. If the answers about waiting list times or lengths are different, be suspicious. Be verrry suspicious. Once the place is yours, then ask the last two questions again to make sure their story hasn't changed and to compare with other managers.

BODY CORPORATES AND SINKING FUNDS

Many apartments, units, terrace houses and other multi-dwelling complexes (including some private town-housing estates) are sold off to individual homeowners or investors by developers—or by investors who can't cope with the massive expense of going-it-alone.

In these situations each unit or dwelling owner will share an interest in the total property valuation, not to mention the building insurance, capital improvements, colour schemes, garden maintenance, tax and council regulation compliances, building repairs, water supply, internet hardwiring and parking problems, to name a few. So a committee—called a body corporate—is elected by the full group of owners to run the day-to-day management of the property. The body corporate also decides how much every share-owner must pay into a 'sinking fund' to pay for day-to-day running costs, while also saving up for long-term improvements and repairs.

Like any legitimate committee, there is a secretary,

president, vice-president, treasurer, annual general meetings, monthly meetings, lots of paperwork and—inevitably—disputes, which can usually only be settled by either negotiation or vote.

Nasty traps:
1. The first year's budget is usually established for the new owners by the property developers (or a company paid by them), so beware of under-estimates of expenses which may be used to attract buyers to their 'bargain' investment.
2. Building faults—however minor—are annoying but commonplace in the first year after construction or after major refurbishment of an old building, and these faults may impact on rent income by loss or temporary relocation of tenants during repairs, even though the repairs themselves may be covered by workmanship warranties. So make sure your budget includes either savings to cope, insurance policies which cover loss of rental income, or a back-up plan for coping with a worst case scenario (see also Cost Benefit Analysis, page 167).
3. Beware of being charged *full* accommodation costs for live-in-managers who would tenant there anyway or who could live nearby in another building for less.
4. Beware of buildings with (or needing) elevators, escalators, swimming pools, gymnasiums, public recreational areas, golf or tennis courts because these increase your body corporate fees for the sinking fund a LOT, without necessarily increasing the amount of rent you get back out of the investment.
5. Beware of investors who are selling off their properties because of arguments with the body corporate. You'll often be buying straight into a fight.

> ### *Did you know?*
> A property investor recently complained to me that she paid massive levies into a sinking fund every month, but then the body corporate—which turned out to be a company who owned most of the building—decided the building needed a makeover that wouldn't clash with their new company colours and logo, so she had to cough up $15,000 extra within 3 months to help pay for their makeover—or be hit with body corporate penalties to pay off (or fight in court).

Handy Hints:
1. When shopping for an investment property, read and compare the body corporate rules thoroughly AND also ask for the minutes from the last three monthly meetings of at least three other multi-dwelling investments, so you can get the hang of the lingo and common practices of a body corporate before committing a big chunk of your financial future to one in particular.
2. Before investing in ANY property that's managed by a body corporate, read the minutes from the last big Annual General Meeting (AGM) and ask if you can sit in on their next ordinary committee meeting BEFORE you sign anything. Committee meetings are usually held monthly, so be suspicious of any body corporate who sets their monthly meetings at a time or place which is difficult for you—or any of its other share-owners—to get to.
3. Avoid ANY investment that deals with share ownership of ANY kind—even if it's with a member of your own family—if you're the type of investor who likes to keep in control, who has poor negotiation skills during time of dispute, or who needs your freedom to buy, sell and manage your investment to meet your changing needs and expectations.

Did you know?

Submissions closed in July 2002 for proposed legislative changes aimed at providing the Ministry of Housing with greater powers to intervene in tenant-landlord disputes, particularly where boarding houses are concerned and to grant boarding house landlords with better conditions for dealing with abandoned belongings, house rules and tenant eviction. Proposed changes also recommend that boarding house landlords can no longer take more than one week's worth of rent as a bond, but that these smaller bonds no longer have to be forwarded to the Tenancy Services Centre.

Handy hint: 'Park' the bonds in your mortgage offset account (aka revolving credit mortgage) and you can save up to $96 in interest for every $10 bond parked in your 30-year mortgage at current interest rates.

The legislation proposes to go even further, impacting on procedures for lodging and disputing bonds. The Tenancy Tribunal also aims to award damages against landlords who fail to comply with building, health or safety regulations arising from shonky housing standards. But most significantly, landlords, rather than tenants, will soon have to pay any letting fee charged by the real estate agents (or property managers) involved in finding tenants for your investment property.

For more information, contact the Ministry for Housing, ph 04 472 2753, or keep half an eye on their website: www.minhousing.govt.nz

11

Your Property Management Plan (PMP)

I can think of a thousand things off the top of my head that I'd rather be doing than paperwork. Can't you? But that's one of the main reasons I always go to the trouble of putting together a Property Management Plan (PMP) and a property management folder each time I start a major new investment. I do them right away, while I'm still pumped with fresh enthusiasm for my new project. And I do them in detail, because a little work now saves you weeks worth of it later.

ADVANTAGES
Organising, goalsetting, monitoring and reporting. A Property Management Plan will make all of these tasks easier. All you're doing in assembling your PMP is compiling all the information you'll be using over and over again. So the first person who benefits from your PMP is you. You'll also be writing up a very brief summary of what you want, when you want it and how you plan to achieve it—no more than a sentence or two is needed under these headings. It's mainly just to get things straight in your own head so you know where you're going and what you have to do to get there.

A PMP will pay for itself because it makes you look professional to a tax auditor, with whom it counts the most. Running an investment in a business-like manner helps to widen the kinds of things you can claim as deductible expenses, especially in the office and with vehicles—but always within reason of course. Also, between your PMP and your diary, you may be able to justify expenses for driving around looking at properties, phone calls to real estate agents, your banks and solicitor as soon as you start looking for your first investment. However, the IRD may only allow you to claim expenses from the date your property is available for letting, if you spend too much in travelling costs or take too long shopping.

Otherwise, many people only manage to claim from the date the property goes under contract. (You can usually claim pre-purchase expenses for up to three months before you sign a property contract without any trouble from the Inland Revenue provided everything is claimed honestly and provided you purchase your investment property within that same financial year. Anything outside those parameters and you'll have to work harder to justify it when you get audited.)

Your bank manager will be interested in seeing your PMP when you apply for your loan. (Especially if they're having second thoughts about approving your loan—because it's tangible evidence that you're serious about succeeding.)

Your accountants will also appreciate your PMP as very few investors bother to put one together, no matter how often they recommend it. Your accountants can use it every year when they do your tax to see where you started the year and where you finished it—in real terms rather than in the dollars and cents columns they're used to seeing. (And very often—if you keep it brief and easy to read—a PMP will help them spot opportunities that could make next year's return even better for you.)

A PMP is also a Godsend to any of your beneficiaries if you earn your angel's wings unexpectedly, because they will not only see at a glance what the property is all about, but also its potential and how to manage it. And everything they need to find, manage or sell will be right there in front of them—especially if you keep this little book inside the folder's front pocket.

WHAT'S IN IT?

Your Property Management Plan consists of one folder for each of the investment properties in your portfolio, and each folder contains:

A title page

Your title page is easy. It simply says 'Property Management Plan' and lists the address of the property and the name(s) of the person(s) who own it.

A contents page

Your file will get bigger as the years go by, so a contents page—and little index tabs on the sides of the different sections, if you want to get really excited—makes everything much easier to find.

An area map

An area map highlighting your property and abutting streets does not only help you to see your property from a pigeon's eye view, you can also fax it to tradespeople or real estate agents whenever you need to organise quotes or inspections to help them find the place. As mentioned earlier, you can get maps which show property boundaries from the real estate agent or sometimes from your local council. Some government departments provide them too, but for a fee, so if you can't get one easily, an enlarged photocopy of your local street directory will do. (Highlight the map reference number, the grid co-ordinates of the street in your latest book of street maps and note which year that book of maps was published.) If you can't find any maps at all, then draw one yourself with brief directions underneath so you can fax the page to anyone if required.

If it's a large block—over an acre—or a steep block, or even a block which you may suspect has been filled and compacted, then I'd also take the precaution of buying a topographical map from the Lands Department to see where the height-above-sea-level lines are and also where the true ground level was—roughly—before anyone played with landfill. (See page 179 for example.)

Photos
Include a photo taken from the street (often available from the real estate agent), a photo of the backyard and/or the back of the house, and photos of every room in the condition that tenants will find them when they move in will also come in handy. Underneath the main photo, add a list of features as you would describe them over the phone to a real estate agent who may wish to manage the place, or to a prospective tenant who may ring up asking about it.

A Property Management Plan sheet
On a clean A4 page, write the title 'Property Management Plan'. Then list the following headings and write one or two brief sentences explaining each topic in relation to YOU and YOUR investment property:

- Motivation: why do you want to invest in property?
- Why this property?: what is special about this property?
- Attributes: what are its best features? (eg. Street appeal, as new condition or proximity to a major Tim Tam supply?)
- Detriments: what do you see as its failings. (eg. Is the yard prone to stormwater flooding, or do the taps hammer when you switch them off too fast?)

- Erosion protection required: list anything you need to do to protect your investment from washing down the hill.
- Contamination protection: list anything you could do to stop poisons washing in from up the street/next door/off your own roof into drinking-water tanks.
- Fertility protection: a healthy yard means a healthy environment for working/living, so list anything you need to do to get the place up to scratch.

An 'objectives and rules' page

This is where you state the rules by which you choose to govern your own investment. I've included my own objectives and rules sheet below to give you an idea. Feel welcome to use it word for word or to adapt it to suit how you feel about your own investment and add or delete your own rules as you see fit. (NOTE: I drew this up for my first property purchase when I was sixteen, and surprisingly, I haven't felt the need to change it yet.)

Property Management Plan
Objectives and Rules Sheet

Objectives
1. To have repaid the loan within 3 years so that the property is debt-free by   /   /   .

2. To generate income and re-invest this into the property in order that it be fully established, maintained and self-funding and earning the greatest income possible by   /   /   .

(NOTE: These dates are usually the same for me. But if the first date is a period of 3 years or more after your loan was started, you may still prefer the second date to be within your first three years of ownership, perhaps from the date where you plan to refinance the loan so that income from the property is enough to repay the loan, without any contributions from you anymore.

3. To ensure the property is managed in such a way as to ensure a perpetual income, whilst minimising the impact on the environment.

Rules
1. MINIMISE DEBT: Take loans as a last resort for only those items that will eventually pay for themselves or that will appreciate in value. Borrow only the minimum amount required at the lowest rate available and repay as fast as possible.
2. START SMALL AND GROW LARGE: Commence earning income as soon as possible and return all generated income into improvements to increase income until the property is at full income-earning capacity.
3. CONTROL EXPENDITURE: Budget income and expenditure over the full establishment period to allow steady growth without risk of loss.
4. SAVE FOR FUTURE REQUIREMENTS: Establish a goal account out of my paypacket to supplement property income for capital expense and to help make repayments during non income-earning periods. Then once the property is debt-free, put 10% of all property income towards superannuation with the rest being split between personal lifestyle improvements and saving up for a deposit on the next investment.

5. **ENSURE PERPETUALITY:** Ensure all buildings including sheds and fences are maintained to a high standard and avoid the use of non-biodegradable chemicals wherever possible to ensure permanent soil health and quality of living environment. Use only ecologically sound fertilisers and pest control. (NOTE: The goal here is to have the property as good in 50 years time as it is now, if not better.)

YOUR QUICK AND EASY GROSS MARGIN ANALYSIS

Gross margin analysis is just a techo accountant's term for a table which forecasts what you think your total gross income will be under various circumstances from bad times to good, minus any costs that vary in direct proportion to the income you get. (eg. If your manager charges you 10% of the weekly rent, then the higher the rent, the more income they earn). Then at the bottom of your report there's a list of all your fixed expected costs, such as rates and advertising to find a tenant, etc.

NOTE: If you're using a financial advisor or purchasing through an investment scheme, network or fund manager, then ask THEM to provide this very basic report for you—as well as the cost benefit report, which follows.

If they don't have them, ask why the heck not, because these reports help you to see at a glance where your potential income and expense blowouts can be.

Don't freak out about getting it exactly right. Your bank manager might appreciate seeing it if he's having second thoughts approving your loan, but you'll be the one who gets the most benefit out of this exercise.

Simply work out a table that looks something like this:

Sample Annual Gross Income Analysis

$Rent/ week	Assuming vacancy rate = zero (all 52 weeks with income)	If vacant 3 weeks in 52 (= income for 49 weeks/ year)	If vacant 6 weeks in 52 (= income for 46 weeks/ year)	If vacant 10 weeks in 52 (= income for 42 weeks/ year)	If vacant 16 weeks in 52 (= income for 36 weeks/ year)
$280	$14560	$13720	$12880	$11760	$10080
$290	$15080	$14210	$13340	$12180	$10440
$300	$15600	$14700	$13800	$12600	$10800
$310	$16120	$15190	$14260	$13020	$11160
$320	$16640	$15680	$14720	$13440	$11520
$330	$17160	$16170	$15180	$13860	$11880
$340	$17680	$16660	$15640	$14280	$12240

NOTE #1: I've calculated this table for a property where rent could reasonably be charged between $280 and $340 per week, based on what a real estate agent may suggest other homes in the area are earning. If your property is in a different income bracket, then simply recalculate the table by multiplying the rent per week by the number of weeks earning income.

Eg. In the vacancy rate = zero column, the first amount is $280 × 52 weeks rented = $14,560.

> There's a blank *Annual Gross Income Analysis* Table on page 233 for your convenience.

NOTE #2: The above example is for someone who manages their property themselves, so they don't really have any expenses that go up or down if the rent changes. This is therefore the simplest form of the table. If you do use a property manager who charges a fee that's calculated as a percentage of the rent per week, then it will be helpful for you to calculate a second table just like this one for their fees based on the rent you get each week. And then you can do a third table which combines the two, so you can see at a glance how much you will get in each rent category, after fees are deducted. (Or simply skip the first two tables and do a table that only has the details of the 'income nett of management fees'. Or use a spreadsheet with macros which calculates the amounts for you—whichever is easier for you.

NOTE #3: If your property produces income from something other than tenants—eg. pot plants, woollen products or even timber rocking horses—then instead of the rent per week column, you'll use a unit cost (eg. $4.00 for a plant that you sell for $4.50 but costs you $0.50 to produce. No GST figures are needed). And instead of the vacancy columns, you'd have the number of pot plants sold in a good year through to a bad year.

Using the report

The gross margin analysis is great for showing you at a glance what your income range for a year could reasonably expect to be. In this case, there's a difference of $7600, which you'd have to have back-up plans to replace out of your own wallet if you're going to be depending on that income to make your repayments!

The difference between the lowest and highest values in your table is how much you need to keep in a goal or savings account each year for emergencies even when the property has long periods without income.

At the bottom of your table, list all the types of expenses you expect or wish to pay on the place every year. Things like: rates, building insurance, manager's fee to find a tenant, paint (exterior and interior), garden plants, mulch and fertilisers, mower fuel, etc. And then just total up the list, and underline your total expected expenses.

Your gross margin analysis can be as simple as that.

Handy hint: Set up your goal/savings account as a mort-gage offset account so that the money effectively reduces the amount of interest you have to pay on the loan, almost as if it had been paid off the loan anyway. Then at the end of the first or second year, you can decide if you wish to reduce the amount you have on stand-by in that account, depending on your income success rate.

YOUR QUICK AND EASY COST BENEFIT ANALYSIS

The cost benefit analysis for your PMP only needs to be a couple of sentences which explain your interpretations and assumptions from the gross margin analysis you've just done.

So simply pick three samples from your table to show yourself, your bank manager, your accountant and the tax auditor the kind of situation you could be in assuming a best-case, worst-case and expected-average situation. No need to panic here though, because you've just done all the calculations. And I've supplied a sample cost benefit analysis below for you to use or adapt so you can scribble up your own page quickly and easily. Once you've done this report, you'll have a better understand-ing of just how much money for repayments is going to have to come out of YOUR pocket.

Sample Cost Benefit Analysis

General: The purpose of this analysis is to create an expectation of income during worst-case, most likely-case and best-case scenarios in general terms. This study will benefit decision-making for management strategies with the aim of ensuring that income is maximised and re-invested into the loan and into capital improvements so that accelerated capital gain benefits are also generated.

Calculation: This cost benefit analysis is based on results from the gross margin analysis, which is also enclosed in this property management plan. When examining these extrapolations (forecasts) it is important to note that income is affected by a large number of variable factors that can influence yields to a large extent and with little or no prior warning. For this reason, the examples below represent only a range of probable outcomes.

Case study one—worst-case scenario

A regular turnover of tenants throughout the year results in four periods of vacancy between tenants, which average four weeks long each before the next tenant moves in. And in each case, the rent has to be dropped to the cheapest end of the price bracket to attract tenants. So at $280 rent per week over 36 weeks of the year, the worst-case expected returns would be:

Annual rent income: $10,080

Case study two—expected norm

A tenant is found and kept for the full year with only three income weeks out of the year lost between tenants, during which time renovations and repairs are organised to maintain an average rental asking price for the property. So at $310 rent per week over 49 weeks earning income from a tenant, average expected income would be:

Annual rent income: $15,190

Case study three—best-case scenario

The house is advertised prior to settlement (or prior to being vacated by the last tenant) and high demand for rental properties in that area and high quality of maintenance and features for this property means that maximum rent can be achieved for the full year with no vacancy weeks at any time. So at $340 per week over 52 weeks, the expected income would be:

Annual rent income: $17,680

NOTE: Income can fluctuate up to 33.6%

End of Report.

YOUR CAPITAL GAIN FORECASTS

This page should come from your financial advisor, property manager or network advisor who was initially responsible for talking you into the investment. Or have a rough (and hopefully very conservative) go yourself by asking your bank to calculate the future value of a term deposit that has the same starting value as the current value of your property, invested at the current rate of inflation (about 2.5%) for five or ten years, with interest compounding every six or twelve months.

These forecasts are always interesting to compare later with how much the property actually earns. Of course, you'd never completely believe any projected income (or rise in valuation) from your advisor/lender if they're in the process of trying to talk you into buying a second property at the time. If expected returns were not achieved, then there are plenty of excuses they can use. But there's no point crying over a floundering investment, so you might as well laugh, learn your lesson and move on.

A full loan forecast

This page of your Property Management Plan is easy to get, but it's the scariest—and sometimes the most motivating—page of all. It's a forecast of the monthly loan status for each and every month of the full loan period.

You use it to double-check your real monthly statements to make sure no repayments go astray—and no extra fees get slipped through—in the first few months. You also use it to keep track of how far ahead your extra repayments are actually getting you. And you use it to stay motivated.

Don't panic at the length of it though. Even a 30-year loan can usually be summarised in less than three pages and you can ask for this report free from either your lender, mortgage broker, financial advisor or investment program manager. Or you can use a loan repayment calculator like the ones on my website www.anitabell.com to generate your own. (Or if you're feeling completely insane . . . ooops, I mean energetic . . . you can do what I did with my first loan: forecast the balance owing at the end of every single fortnight after each repayment is due to be transferred.)

Regardless of how you get it, the report will look something like this:

Loan forecasts for the property situated at: 66 Sandwich St, Sandgate.

Principal loan amount = $150,000   Interest rate = 6.5%

Term of loan = 30 years. Settlement date = 10/7/2002

Last repayment due = 12/07/2032

Monthly repayment date	Repayment amount	Interest due	Balance still owing	Total interest paid so far
10/7/01	0	0	$150,000	0
10/8/02	$948	$812	$149,864	$ 812
10/9/02	$948	$811	$149,728	$1624
10/10/02	$948	$811	$149,590	$2435
10/11/02	$948	$810	$149,453	$3245

etc, until the last payment, where the 'interest due' will be close to zero, the balance owing will be a portion of a repayment and the total interest paid will be absolutely mind-boggling. ($191,316!!)

You should also do **a second loan forecast, using the term in which you WISH** to pay off the property (still ensuring that the actual term of the loan you get is the full 25 or 30 years for safety reasons). Then you use this second report so you can see what your self-decided grand-total repayments per month should be AND so you can forecast your financial position at any month in advance AND so you can double-check your actual loan statements for any errors as they come in.

YOUR PROPERTY GOAL SUMMARY

This page of your Property Management Plan is simply a list of things you would like to do to the property to fix it up or improve it so you can ask the highest possible rent. Do a goal sheet at the end of each financial year so you know where you're going at all times, putting the coming year at the top of it and ticking everything off as you achieve it.

Suggested goals for a new property might include: building a toddler-proof fence to keep the backyard safe for youngsters, paving the driveway, repairing an almost leaky roof, adding a carport for vehicle shelter, upgrading the front gardens for street appeal or replacing curtains and carpet in any rooms required. Then you can add a pledge or note at the bottom that goes something like: 'Any project not completed in the current financial year shall be carried forward and prioritised appropriately amongst the next year's goals.'

PLANT AND EQUIPMENT INVENTORY

This report should be split up into two pages. One is for inventory like whipper-snippers, lawn mowers, mulch-makers and computers that you will use in the management and maintenance of all eventual properties in your portfolio.

Your second page of inventory is of all the 'stealable' equipment which is actually kept at the property. Things like dishwashers, refrigerators, floor polishers, and anyhing else you provide to help tenants look after your investment.

At the bottom of each inventory page, include a list of inventory that you'd like to save up for and note how much you think each of them will cost.

Handy hint #1: Also note at which address each item is ordinarily stored. For example, it may be easier to keep your ride-on mower for a large property at a friend's house nearby if you don't trust the tenants with it. NOTE: Keeping this record is not only helpful as your memory fades as you get older and can't remember where you've left things, but it's also extremely helpful to an executor of your Will, who has to find everything so they can carve up your estate after you've kicked the bucket.

Handy hint #2: Buying these expensive things for regular use in your rental homes makes them deductible items for tax purposes. Yes, you can use them in your own home too—you can even start depreciating expensive equipment you already have at home, IF you use it regularly to maintain your investment property. But you'll have to work out what percentage is for private use and make sure you don't depreciate that by accident. Ask your accountant or the Inland Revenue (ph 0800 377 774) for details.

Handy hint #3: Check the property thoroughly and start your inventory of equipment as soon as you've signed the contract. If it's electrical and only plumbed in or bolted down, it can be easily taken by owners or real estate agents, so make sure it's mentioned on the contract as an inclusion and make sure it's actually in the house on the day of handover. If anything is missing, report it to the police immediately. (Very often, the only people who know what's been mentioned on a contract and what's usually supposed to go with a sold property are the real estate agent, the owner and you, so the culprit shouldn't be too hard to find.)

Handy hint #4: Supply your property manager with a list of inventory to be ticked off at each regular inspection, signed and dated.

A copy of the contract to buy the place
Your solicitor will keep a copy in a safe place for you. But it helps to have one on hand when you need it, so I keep one copy in my PMP. (I also keep the original in another file for my growing stack of original contracts.) Even if you never need to look at your purchase contract again over the many years that you own the block, the details from it come in very handy again when it's time to sell.

A copy of the mortgage documents
These are the papers you get from the bank containing schedules of all your fees and charges. Your accountant will need a copy of these to calculate which of your start-up costs can be written off and which need to be depreciated or taken care of later. But you may need these documents later too, since they contain all the terms and conditions of your loan—including any penalties you need to be aware of before doing anything out of the ordinary.

A copy of any important correspondence from your solicitor
You may need this later if problems arise.

A copy of your first and annual loan statements
Your first loan statement has a full and official record of all fee transactions, so I always keep a copy of that in the PMP too. I also ask for an annual statement at the end of every financial year (provided there is no ridiculous fee involved. These are in addition to all monthly statements you get, by the way, because you'll be filing those with your annual tax records—whereas your PMP is more like a perpetual file that you use year after year.)

YOUR END OF FINANCIAL YEAR REPORTS
Even if you only have one property in your portfolio, you can still benefit from writing up an official annual report—just like a major investment company. But it's

nothing to flip-out over. You can get away with a single page of comments which basically just detail your achievements or anything that stopped you from doing what you wanted to in the last financial year.

I usually split up my very brief comments under headings like:

- *Forecast accuracy:* Where I jot notes about the accuracy of my forecasts. If they were out, I write why I think it happened and what I can do to stop it happening next time.
- *Income report:* Where I write only one or two sentences about tenant turnover, or other income produced from the property and if it could have been done better then I jot notes on how I would like to try doing it.
- *Expense report:* Where I scribble a sentence or two about any major purchases or expenses required and note how much loan interest I paid for the year.
- *Other changes:* Where I note any changes to the investment in general; for example a change in town zoning, in rateable values or in debt structuring if I refinanced with the same or another lender. If new services, industry or roadworks have come into the area which could affect the potential income from the property, then that will rate a mention here too.
- *Management associations:* Where I note who my accountants, property managers and solicitors were that year (and no, I don't really change them that often, but it helps to keep those records for when I do).
- *Problems:* Where I note any of the agents, banks or businessmen that I'll never use again.
- *Conclusion:* To remind me in future years of how well or lousy I felt my investment performed that year in particular (eg. 'Generally happy with tenants, but the property manager needed a kick in the pants too often for my liking. Returns: as predicted. Expenses were a

little high with the roller-door getting stuck on the back bumper of that run-away Ferrari, but a change of building insurer from ABC Limited to XYZ Incorporated has reduced my premium excess to $150 instead of $550. Better luck next time.')

Then sign and date it.

Copies of any valuations
You may be able to get your first valuation from your lender—if they're agreeable—by asking them for a copy of the valuation report you paid for with your loan application fees. Or you can sometimes get one from a real estate agent for free when you list the property for sale or to rent. Or you could try a registered valuer, but you'll have to pay them for the information. You might also like to include a copy of each rate notice where the unimproved value of the land changes up or down to what it was in the previous period.

Your completed investment property checklist
It's always interesting to keep the checklists you used in selecting your property. Some of the properties may be for sale again (or still) the next time you're ready to buy again.

A copy of the welcome sheet
Keep the original of your welcome sheet for tenants here in case the copy from the house goes missing and you need to photocopy and laminate another one.

Copies of any disclosure statements
Disclosure statements should advise buyers of any ongoing obligations, body corporate fees or undertakings that all renovations made by the current or future owners will suit the style of the whole complex/development etc. These usually only apply to units or townhouses where owners are

obligated to manage or maintain the property to a certain standard, and if applicable, they should have been given to you through the real estate agent by the vendor BEFORE you signed any contract or paid any deposit.

You'll have to provide these in turn to your buyer when it's your turn to sell, so keep copies of the ones you were given safe in your PMP. It makes signing one when you need to sell so much easier—especially if you're selling by private sale.

A copy of any agreement or contract with your property manager
You'll need to refer to this if ever there's any trouble.

A copy of the tenancy agreement, signed by tenants
This one will be useful if you need to check your rights before doing anything out of the ordinary, as well as for reference to if there's trouble.

A page of business cards for local tradesmen
These are always handy in the event of an emergency or even regular repairs.

A list of advertising methods used, with notes about the success rate
You'll only find this one useful if you're managing the property yourself. Sometimes you could go for years with the same tenants, and remembering which advertising was effective is next to impossible. So it's helpful to keep notes on where you got the best response from advertising each time you have to do it, so you don't waste money on ineffective advertising for that property next time.

A copy of any sole or exclusive agency documents
You sign these when you're ready to re-sell the place, and you'll need to keep track of their expiry dates so keep

them in your PMP folder if your property is on the market for longer than two months.

Master section
If you have more than one property, you can use a larger ring binder, with a master section at the front for paperwork that applies to all properties. (eg. your master goal sheet, inventory of equipment that you use for maintenance in all properties, and your annual reports etc.)

Alternatively, you can have separate folders for each property, plus a master folder, which you always keep filed with the others. It's your choice, depending on how big your portfolio is, how big your folder is getting, and how organised you want all your records to be.

TOPOGRAPHICAL MAPS—OPTIONAL
Get a topographical map of your local area from your local authority (or valuer, if you hire one), remembering that the purchase of the map is tax deductible.

Make sure the map includes the height-above-sea-level. Then look at which height lines go over your property. (The lines on official maps usually only have numbers on them, but the word 'metres' is usually implied.)

In the following example for one of my bigger blocks, you can see that the lowest points above sea level are 75 m and the highest points are 80 m above sea level. The lines are far apart but only 5 m in difference, so you can see that this block is nearly flat, but slopes away from the road towards the creek—just as you might guess that it would. You can also tell from the map that there is a circle of land that's 80 m above sea level near the road and that there are three powerpoles nearby it on the street, so the topographical map is instantly helpful in showing the best place to put any buildings—on that highest spot, of course. The future building site then tells us the best place to put a driveway entrance and gate.

Since this topographical map is to scale, the number of powerpoles along the street gives you a rough idea of this property's size. Also note that this map is a photocopied enlargement of only one property from a topographical map that encompassed over five entire suburbs. During enlargement, I had to erase much of the irrelevant details so I could add my own.

The hand-drawn features you see look as if they were drawn directly onto the map, but in fact, they were drawn onto clear plastic sheets which I labelled 'topography' and 'improvements'. I arranged these so they folded down in different layers so I could draw plans of desired features and see how they worked with existing features *before* spending any money on them. The afforestation project to prevent further erosion in the washouts along the creek was therefore planned on a separate clear plastic sheet according to the height-above-sea-level lines—before I turned over a single sod of soil.

I also had a full page grid on a third plastic sheet—not shown here—that was to scale with the underlying property map, so I could overlay the grid over the map and work out areas and distances with barely half a glance—a fantastic time and money saver if you're trying to work out large soil or mulch volumes or plant numbers without being able to measure them exactly.

And that's all there is to it. It sounds like a big list, I know, but your PMP folder is just full of stuff you'll get and need to find a filing space for anyway—and your usual shoebox won't be big enough. There's only a handful of pages to write up yourself, and hopefully, I've made even those as fast and easy as possible for you.

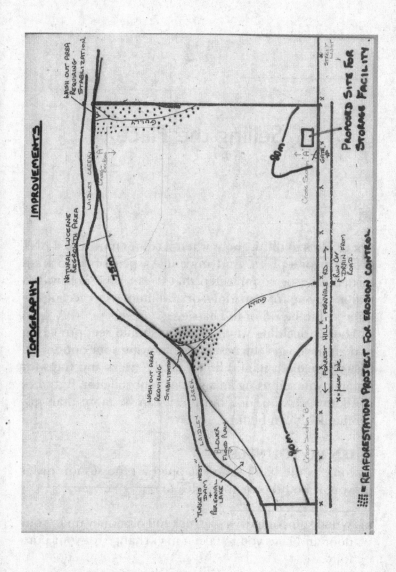

12

Selling the Place

There's lots to think about when it comes time to sell ANY property for a profit. And any single aspect of it can seem so daunting or complicated that it can leave you with a major craving for Panadol—or a willingness to accept any offer just to be rid of the hassle.

There's deciding when or if you should sell, preparing to do it so you get the best price, knowing your options on how to go about it, and finally all the tricks and traps for doing it yourself using an agent or your solicitor. But once you know what to look out for, it can be more than just profitable. It can be fun.

WHEN DO YOU SELL?
As long as the bank hasn't slapped a repossession order on you, it would be a good idea to sell:

a) When someone drives a truck full of money up to your door and begs you to take it in exchange for your portfolio.
b) When you get sick of managing tenants, managers, maintenance and repairs and want to invest in something that requires little or no effort.

c) When the valuation and/or equity goes up so much in one property that you can sell it and buy two properties in another growth area for no greater expense.

d) When the valuation and/or equity goes up so much that you can sell it, pay out your own home and still have money left over for a big deposit on a new investment.

e) When your income drops and you need to lower your total repayments or restructure your debt in order to survive safely.

f) When you've done well, but can smell nasty election policies coming.

g) When you're struggling to keep making repayments, but the bank doesn't know how hard it is yet.

PRICE-SAVVY PRESENTATION

Before listing a property for sale, it's wise to get it looking its best and keeping it that way until someone signs a contract to buy it. Obviously, the less you spend, the higher your returns, but don't scrimp on repairs or clean-up jobs that could help achieve a faster sale for you (and probably for a better price). Remember that every day you owe money on a loan is costing you money at the rate of not only the interest and monthly fees you have to pay, but also the interest your funds could have been earning if they were invested elsewhere.

Every day that you own the place is also one day more that you have to pay building insurance, rates, phone connection, insurance policies and mortgage protection for it. It's also one day less that you could be investing somewhere else for greater capital growth. So obviously, price-savvy presentation will reap more rewards than you may imagine and once you decide to sell, you should aim to sell quickly.

Handy hints
- Scrub down the exterior walls and eaves with high

pressure water and soap, then stand back to see if you can get away without a fresh touch-up paint job at the front (where buyers get their first impression).

- Clear all weedy-looking plants out of the gardens, trim any straggly branches and re-mulch garden beds so they look tidy and easy to care for. Mow the lawn with the blades up about 5 cm off ground level, then chuck a box of weed'n'feed over the front lawn (and the back lawn too if you can). Then hose it in, so the lawn grows higher, lusher and is softer to walk on. (This encourages better roots, so it should look greener and healthier too.) Don't underestimate the first impressions of a tidy green lawn. Short, brown or crunchy lawns are a major turn off (subconsciously, where it counts), so a little extra effort will cost you little, but can earn you a faster sale at a higher price, if the house is also kept tidy.

- Get rid of dead or dying pot plants inside and out. Clean pet areas of smelly poo corners. Hose down flyscreens for cobwebs, then call pest control to evict all tenants that have six or more legs. (Remember to ask your exterminator to keep watch for signs of termites as they spray around outside and ask them to note on your receipt if they see any *obvious* evidence of them or not.)

- If you have tenants, ask them to keep kitchen benches tidy, floors swept and garbage outside, secured neatly in bins. Also ask them to take down any underwear hanging from ceiling fans, to keep basins clear of leg hair and whiskers, toilets flushed (don't laugh, some don't!) and their dogs and cats smelling like roses if they can't be kept outside.

> **Handy hint**
> A little car wash or polish in the high pressure water stream will often clear oxidised paint off exterior house walls fast and easily. But try a small section first where it can't be seen in case it strips the paint.

NOTE: For this kind of inconvenience, you may like to offer free rent for your tenants the last week as an incentive to help you get a fast sale . . . or maybe you can think of something more appropriate to their personal interests?

- Arrange deodorisation of carpets if you can smell them as you walk in. If your tenants smoke, try asking them not to do it when buyers are around—or to (please) keep windows open and breezy.
- If the house is fitted with a waste water recycling pit and/or a septic tank, then dose all toilets and kitchen drains with Actizyme to get them working properly (or use a similar non-hazardous bio-degrade accellerant, available from Mitre 10 or Placemakers) so that contents are decomposing properly and buyers don't get knocked over by any obnoxious odours while they're outside.

YOUR OPTIONS ON HOW TO SELL

The next step to selling your investment property is deciding how you're going to do it. If you have the time, energy and the facilities to produce eye-catching posters for community noticeboards, then doing it yourself can save you approximately 4% of the sale price on commissions that you'd otherwise have to pay if you went through an agent. Of course, you also need good negotiation skills (or a fair price that you can justify and stick to) or else you could lose all your savings by having to sell for a much lower price than you may have achieved through an agent. If the thought of DIY scares you, you can use an agent with an open listing by multi-listing through various agents, or by signing agreements for either sole agency or an exclusive sale—all of which have their own little tips and snags to be wary of.

DO IT YOURSELF

If you're not rushed to sell, you might try DIY for a short time before listing it through an agent. Two to three months should be enough time for you to either succeed with a profit or give up in disgust.

NOTE: Most REIs discourage amateur vendors from attempting the sales tasks of a licensed professional—especially when they're dealing with their most valuable asset; and to a large extent where amateurs are concerned, I agree. But just because you find a buyer, doesn't mean you have to sign a contract.

If you find a buyer who tries to bully you into a lower price or slacker conditions, there's nothing stopping you from walking into your nearest reputable real estate agent with the property details in one hand and the potential buyer's details in the other and saying: 'Hey, guys, if you can get a better price out of this buyer than what I've got now, I'll split the difference with you.' With no legwork or advertising for the agent, they'd be silly not to try—although they may want your offer to them in writing. If they fail, you're no worse off. You'll probably be sick of the whole DIY process by then anyway, and if your buyer bails out on you, you'll have just found an agent who deserves first bite of your listing opportunity.

Warning #1: At the time of writing, REINZ member agents and solicitors contribute deposits and other monies to a Fidelity Fund through which buyers and/or sellers can claim compensation if either party suffers difficulties or financial loss during a transaction under certain circumstances. But if a private seller conducts the transaction, then neither party will be eligible to make a claim through this fund. So that's a trap both buyers and sellers need to be wary of. (By the way, if you're *buying* a property privately, make sure you get signed approval from ALL owners that they agree to the property being sold BEFORE you sign a contract. The last thing you want is to pay application fees for a loan on a property where the husband didn't even know his home was for sale.

Warning #2: If you have a real estate agent handling the rent collection, then check your agreement with them *first* before attempting to sell the place because they may have a line of fine print that allows them first opportunity to make the listing. Don't leave yourself open to being sued for commission that wasn't earned. If you have to pay them, they might as well work hard for it.

Warning #3: Potential buyers can be just as annoying as bad tenants, so don't attempt DIY unless your whole family is ready to back you for the full effort. Try offering your partner and kids a share in the rough equivalent of commission you'll be saving. (Or help them spend it later on something the whole family can enjoy after settlement —like a new swimming pool, TV entertainment system or holiday.) Since agent commissions typically cost between $4000 and $20,000 per sale—depending on the sale price and percentage you're charged—you should be able to afford something generous and still have great savings to spare!

Handy tips for DIY: Use a PC with colour printer to run off eye-catching 'for sale' posters that have detachable 'fingers' along the bottom with your contact number. (That way potential buyers can tear off your number and take it home.) Posters should be ½ or ⅓ of A4 size paper so they won't hog noticeboards. (Noticeboard hogs get buried or taken down.) Community noticeboards can be found at shopping centres, gymnasiums, libraries and church halls, or you could try asking service stations and corner stores if they'll permit your poster in their window. Do all of this for at least three suburbs in all directions from the property. Then jot a list of points that you didn't include on your flyer to keep beside the phone so you can interest callers further when they ring. (Internet selling tips: see page 73.)

Allow yourself an advertising budget of up to 0.01% of the price you hope to achieve and

> Yes, DIY is a lot of leg-work if you want a fast sale, but you have to make up for the fact that you don't have an office where buyers are going to come looking for you.

spend it placing ads in weekend newspapers and real estate magazines (check out your newsagent for latest mags). Ask for discounts for running ads on multiple weekends and remember that you won't get access to any money from the sale—not even the deposit—until AFTER settlement, so also ask for monthly advertising accounts if possible, so you're not out of pocket too long between placing the ad and selling the property.

Fine-tune your sales skills by shifting your perspective to see your property through the eyes of a buyer. As you speak to them, try to figure out what their needs are and then show them how the property fulfils these needs—WITHOUT being too pushy or obvious about it. As naïve as this may sound, honesty has always been my best policy.

Don't try to hide or bodgy any obvious faults. Instead, ask them if they want you to make repairs of any problems included in the price, or if they would prefer you to drop the price by the value of materials so they can do it them-selves. Or show how a fair amount has already been deducted from the asking price so they can choose and arrange repairs to suit themselves.

For DIY, you'll also need a blank contract. If your buyers are organised and serious, they'll provide one for you with their offer which may include extra clauses which they've already discussed with their solicitor. But if you need a blank contract to fill in with them, or to compare with their offer, ask your solicitor for a new one or look

Handy hints for justifying the asking price of ANY property

If buyers try to negotiate a lower price than you wish to go, try justifying your price with:

- **The last valuation done.** Try to get a copy from your lender each time you refinance. Some lenders will refuse to release the information, but if they do give it to you, store it in your property management folder. Otherwise, start with the unimproved value of your land from your rates notice and add on the replacement value of everything that sits on the land.

- **Pest control report.** You should be asking your annual contractor to keep an eye out for signs of termites and wood borers each time they treat your investment property for spiders, ants and other nasties. But a buyer will be worried about organising this report once the place goes under contract, so providing copies of your report and treatment history will help remove that worry and will help you to justify a good price for a good property.

- **Evidence of council approvals** for all extensions and outbuildings. If it's officially approved, then you can show how everything was done to a high standard, therefore justifying your price.

- **Evidence of warranties** for anything you've bought or had built will transfer to the new owners if you provide them with copies of receipts. (If receipts have been lost, give them a schedule of details including the product, who you bought it from, when, for how much and whose name you bought it under.) Tally up the value of everything under warranty including ovens, hot water systems, buildings, sheds and pumps etc. Then present this to buyers as potential savings if any of those items need repair.

back on the original contract that you used to buy the property in the first place. (Remember that you have a copy in your Property Management Plan.)

Handy hint: Don't muck around with a private sale too long if it's not working. The sooner you get the money from this sale, the sooner you can move on to bigger and better things.

CHOOSING YOUR AGENT—FOR SELLING

Choosing an agent to handle the sale of your surplus property isn't quite the same as choosing the agent who helped you buy it—especially if they were really helpful in getting you the lowest price because they're not likely to be the best agent to get the highest price for it now. (It's a hard trick indeed for agents to please both buyers and sellers at the same time!) You'll probably have to settle for a happy medium, but you can help tilt the scale in your direction by checking out the agent's profile from your new perspective as a seller.

One way to establish an agent's profile is to look at the weekend newspapers and see which agency seems to be marketing their listings effectively. Who has the best ads with the most honest descriptions and interesting points highlighted?

Sellers who want the absolute top price may be tempted to use agents who are vague about prices and features, so they can work their salesmanship 'magic' on unsuspecting buyers. Ads placed by these agents are laced with words like 'price on application' or 'it's *so* affordable, ring now!'

But I've found that such agents will usually try to work their same salesmanship 'magic' on the fees and commission scales they charge YOU. Everyone gets bitten. To sleep better at night, I therefore look for agents who advertise properties with pictures, prices and main features clearly and honestly declared. Then I'd ask friends, family, workmates, neighbours or nearby business-people for their personal recommendations of good agents for sellers in that area.

Next step is to ring the agents with a few questions. Make sure they're a member of the Real Estate Institute so you know they must conduct themselves under an approved code of ethics. (And report them if they don't!) REINZ members also attend regular seminars to ensure they're up with current legislation and they'll be covered by professional indemnity insurance if there's an accident while you're out in their care.

RATES OF COMMISSION

It used to be that the Real Estate Institute would recommend a maximum commission rate (or sliding scale) for their members so vendors were protected from getting ripped off by escalating charges. But in the mid-'90s, deregulation of the real estate industry meant this level of protection was chucked out the window in favour of an almost-anything-goes-depending-on-the-market method. Now, you are usually able to negotiate commission scales when you're comparing agents.

Some offices thankfully still publish their recommended commission rates, while others will still tell you what the current going rate is (very roughly). So if you're a learner-vendor, at least you have some kind of benchmark to tell just how badly you're being ripped off—or how much you're saving—whenever you negotiate. Also, many member agents (in offices where rates are still recommended) will still try to insist on adhering to them. So while you may not get the best deal on commission without taking the matter up with the owner of that agency for an individual negotiation, at least you know you won't be completely ripped off either.

THE LATEST JUICY INFO FROM YOUR REI

The Real Estate Institute of New Zealand has a great website at www.reinz.co.nz which provides links to their associates at Real Estate New Zealand (realenz.org.nz) and between them, the two websites provide links to every-thing you'll need to know about buying and selling all kinds of property in every area of New Zealand (with some links also applicable to overseas).

If you have internet access, these websites can provide you with the latest juicy info about the real estate industry as well, with hours of interesting reading and property listings to drool over. For Kiwis interested in making the hop to Australia, you'll find plenty more to interest you on the following websites too:

(NOTE: Some Real Estate Institutes in Australia have websites tailored to provide information to members only, but the following websites have all their latest juicy info available to everyone for free.)

In Queensland try www.reiq.com.au; In Western Australia try www.reiwa.com.au

And the national website at www.reiaustralia.com.au has some interesting general info on it too—enough to shock the wool from off your eyes, especially when it comes to all the extra stamp duties you have to pay over there.

ENGAGING THE SERVICES OF YOUR REAL ESTATE AGENT

Before signing any 'selling agreement' with your real estate agent, you'll have to provide evidence that you have the full legal right to sell the property.

You will need: A copy of your last rates notice, your driver's licence as proof of identity, as well as your last loan statement and sometimes the original approval letter for your loan as well.

As soon as you've chosen your agent(s), you'll need to sign an authority which gives them the right to list the property for sale. You'll need to provide an exact property description so they don't put details of your neighbour's property on the sale-contract by mistake. But don't panic, as this info should be on your last rates notice as well as on the approval letter for your loan.

Your agent will visit the property with you in order to:	Hints to prepare you:
• Discuss their commission.	Talk to other agents about their commissions first.
• Discuss presentation.	Clean up outside and make sure inside is neat so the place looks tidy and easy to care for.
• Sight or take original rates notice and mortgage papers to photocopy and return.	Be prepared. Have copies ready for them to take away, so your originals can't get lost.
• Assess and advise you of their valuation of your property.	Check the valuation when you last re-financed, ask to see sale reports of other houses in your area, or as a last resort, pay for an independent valuation if you doubt their suggested price range.
• Offer you choices for your marketing plan.	Some agents demand large up-front advertising fees. Others book up thousands in magazine ads that get deducted from the buyer's deposit at settlement or when the property is withdrawn from sale. But I prefer agents who set limits on advertising and deduct it only if they make the sale, with options for extra advertising pre-paid as desired.
• Ask you to sign a disclosure statement for potential buyers—if applicable. (See page 175 for details.)	Copies of these documents should already be in your property management folder from when you bought the place.

• Ask you to finalise minor repairs.	Claim as many repairs against insurance, warranty or your current/last tenant's bond as you can, paying for them yourself first on credit card to maximise your rewards points at the same time as you use your interest-free period (up to 55 days if applicable), so it doesn't cost you any interest.
• Ask you about hours of access.	If you have a dog guarding empty premises or if your tenants have a dog, you may have to buy it a nice chain, or give it a holiday somewhere else, or perhaps ask that all the inspections are done by appointment only. If you do have current tenants check your tenancy agreement, as you may have to do it this way anyhow.

CONVEYANCING AND LAND TRANSFER FEES

Land transfer fees would come to about $150. And legal costs would come in around $500 to $1200, depending on whether you have a mortgage or not. For details, contact your solicitor or the REINZ (contact details on p. 234).

SOLE OR EXCLUSIVE AGENCY

Signing an agreement with your agent for sole or exclusive agency limits you to listing that property through that agent-team only. Under a sole agency agreement, the vendor can still sell the property by their own efforts without owing the agent any commission. But under an exclusive agency arrangement, the seller will have to pay the agent their commission regardless of how the property is sold during the life of the agreement.

The idea of sole or exclusive agency listings are that they're supposed to make your agency work harder as a team, knowing that their efforts won't be wasted by another agency bagging a buyer before them. It defies logic sometimes, because you'd think that the more agencies handling your property, the more potential buyers you'll get. But after trying it both ways, sole agency is the arrangement that I reluctantly prefer, as long as advertising is mostly on a no-sale, no-pay basis.

Warning #1: Agents may be able to sue you for their commission if you make arrangements for a private sale—before or sometimes after the period of their agreement—IF they were responsible for originally introducing the buyers to your property.

Warning #2: Buyers can be shifty and try to secure a cheaper sale price by cutting out the agent. They may tell you they've never been to your agent's office—even if they have—or they may have seen your house advertised in one of your agent's catalogues or windows, or they may have just seen the agent's sign on the front fence. Either way, a court may decide that the agent has introduced the buyers through efforts which must be paid for by commission as set down under the agreement.

Solution: Always check with your sole agent first if they know the people who are trying to contract with you privately, before signing any private contracts. To be extra safe, ask your solicitor if you should provide your agent with the buyer's names in writing (without addresses or contact phone numbers, in case your agent tries to steal them). Say in writing that you have been approached by private buyers with a private offer, and that you would like to honour your sole agency agreement, so you need your agent's prompt reply stating whether they introduced the buyers to your property at any time. For the record, you can also add a note advising how the buyers found out about your place. But keep your solicitor briefed at every stage and seek their advice if the agent hints at trouble.

Handy hint: If you switch from a multi-list to sole agency, contact all agents who had previously listed the property before you signed the sole or exclusive agency agreement, and ask them to sign a note that says you withdrew the property from their listings on such and such a date—or get your sole agent to sign for a list of the agents you've used so they can do it and the onus is on them. Otherwise, your sole agent may be able to sue you for their commission if your property is sold by any other agent while their sole or exclusive agency agreement is in effect.

Never sign a sole or exclusive agency agreement for an indefinite or excessively long period. Two to three months should be plenty. If they work hard for you, you can always sign another agreement when that one runs out if the place hasn't sold by then.

(File copies of all agreements in your property management folder.)

MULTI-LIST AGREEMENTS

This is where your agent agrees to work with another agent in order to sell your property and they agree to share the commission amongst themselves. Any agent can approach a multi-list agent if they have a buyer for a property which they know is for sale. But there's not much stopping them from approaching an agent who has sole or exclusive agreement either, as long as they're both willing to share the commission. However, it's only worth the effort on valuable properties. (For your average suburban residence, you can't blame agents for being reluctant to share commissions if they've put in a lot of leg-work trying to sell them.)

AUCTIONS

If your investment property isn't selling as quickly as you'd like, you may be tempted to sell it by auction. Agents have told me that all the extra advertising—payable on top of any other fees I may have forked out for—is bound to draw a buyer. I've also been told that agencies work much harder to sell properties through auction because they have deadlines. And they usually suggest that excitement and peer pressure on the day can drive prices higher than anything I might have listed the place for to begin with.

But many people go to auctions looking for bargains, which is the last thing you want if you're trying to maximise your capital return. Also, agents should work hard to sell your place no matter how it's listed. And any advertising that occurs will advertise the agency as much as it does for your property, but expenses for it will come entirely out of YOUR pocket—and that's whether the property actually sells at the auction or not.

So you'll have to weigh up how quickly you need to sell, how popular it's likely to be amongst buyers and whether or not you'll get enough extra out of the sale to cover the extra advertising that's necessary in advance of the auction.

> ### Did you know?
> At one of the first auctions I ever went to—a mortgagee auction—the auctioneer only managed to drive the price up to $43,000 when the place was obviously worth almost triple that. I felt very sorry for the vendors, because I saw the 'lucky' buyers later that night at a restaurant in town—and their 3-year-old toddler ran up to the auctioneer when he walked in and said, 'Hi, Uncle John!'

You should also know that selling by auction is a type of exclusive agency agreement and is therefore usually subject to a shorter and stricter agreement period—rarely more than two months, during which time the agent organises effective mass marketing to maximise the number of bidders who are likely to turn up on the day. The first catch is that advertising costs usually have to be paid either up front or soon after the auction, and in either case, that's regardless of whether the property is sold as a result of the auction or not. The second catch is that commission has to be paid if the property sells either before, during, or for an agreed period after the auction.

Often bidders show up looking for a bargain. Vendors show up nervous for a quick sale to help justify their extra auction expenses. So bids usually start low and the auctioneers try to work them upwards—which works to a certain extent, but certainly isn't my idea of a stress-free way of maximising your capital gain.

OPEN LISTING

An open listing is where the seller lists their property with a number of real estate agents in the local area. Each agent can either sell the property individually or work with another agent to sell it. But only the agent who introduces the buyer to the property will receive the commission at settlement date. You could therefore forgive an agent for not supporting this option very much.

ADVERTISING COSTS

Too many agents these days are demanding large upfront advertising fees, whether they sell your properties or not. Some will charge you for addition to their websites, but I like to avoid these guys like the plague. (I know of at least one agency that made more money out of advertising fees one year than it did out of selling properties.)

Handy hint: Before agreeing to hand over hefty advertising fees, ask for contact phone numbers or addresses of up to five clients they've listed that way in the last month and call to see if they're happy with the response/service.

'FOR SALE' SIGNS AND OTHER ADVERTISING

I like to insist that any property I sell is listed *without* a 'for sale' sign tacked to it. Yes, that does cut down the number of people likely to ring the agent. But it has never seemed to raise the number of genuine lookers on those few occasions that I've succumbed to an agent's pleas and consented to a 'for sale' sign being nailed up for a trial period.

'For sale' signs usually look tacky. Unless they're wrought iron or steel-framed jobs that are professionally painted and hung, I think they make even a neatly presented property look cheap and uncared for—especially when they're hung crooked (or start to breed in the front yard). They're also an intrusion on the privacy of the residents. Casual lookers will stop to waste your time (or your tenant's time) with questions, without any real intention to buy it. And neighbours can annoy you with speculations about why you have to sell.

'For sale' signs can also be dangerous on windy days. They're only temporarily tacked up so they occasionally fly off—usually in the direction of parked cars, joggers or windows. And worst of all, 'for sale' signs are sleazebag magnets. They attract the kind of scummy creeps who wait for 'under contract' stickers to go up, so they can steal anything that's not nailed down—and many things that are—as soon as it looks like one lot of owners has moved out.

Agents will try to convince you to permit a sign—some will even insist that it's company policy. But that's because these signs advertise the agency as much as they advertise your property. On one property I owned near the limit of an agent's area, the 'for sale' signs were posted at each end of my 1km main road frontage for a trial period of six weeks. During that time, the agent confessed to getting dozens of inquiries which I later discovered had resulted in at least seven sales of *other* properties without selling mine. It wasn't until a few months after the signs were taken down that my property sold WITHOUT a single 'for sale' sign in sight.

Also—and just as surprisingly—of all the properties I've ever purchased, only one of them has ever had a 'for sale' sign on it. The others were either rented at the time I looked at them, were still in the process of being listed, or were properties that had been listed for a long time and their signs had either blown away or been taken down. (Perhaps by a frustrated vendor or by an agent who didn't like to advertise that the property was taking so long to sell.)

What matters more than a 'for sale' sign on the gate is a photo of the house which appears:

a) in the front window of your agent's office
b) in the property guides or newsletters distributed free to property buyers through various real estate agents, newsagencies and some lenders
c) in at least two weekend newspaper editions for little or no fee

WHAT TO DO WITH YOUR TENANTS

This can be a toughie. Tenants who have been really well-behaved for years can turn hyper-nasty—and creative in their destruction—if they're only given a week or two's notice that the place has been sold, when they're usually entitled to a minimum of four weeks' notice.

So the first thing you have to do is double-check your tenancy agreement to see how much notice you HAVE to provide them with (sometimes it can be even more than the required minimum). Then read the fine print to find out what kind of penalties apply to you if you fail in your obligations. And then make your decision based on how well the tenants have behaved over the time they've been in your house.

NOTE: Highlight your obligations on a copy of your tenancy agreement and add it to your property management folder so you can find the details easily when you need them.

If your tenants have lived like tip rats or been uncooperative or unreliable in making payments, then you'll probably feel justified in not telling them until you absolutely have to, because they could take off in the dead of night, owing you big bucks in rent and repairs. Even if you do have insurance, you'll want to make sure you're covered for deliberate destruction, because the rental bond is rarely worth the kind of damage caused by toxic tenants in even a single room.

> **Warning**
>
> Always ensure that tenants are moved out completely on the day that they are supposed to be. Visit the property yourself to verify this if you have to, because if they've invited friends to stay over after they've moved out, you could find yourself with squatters who are next to impossible to evict. See your solicitor immediately if this happens.

If they've been okay, with rent paid mostly on time and only a few claims requested for repairs to rollerdoors, security systems, hot water systems or the like, then you'll still have to be careful. If you give them extra notice that the house is on the market, then they could start looking for another place ahead of time and leave you with an empty house that's not earning anything while it's still waiting to be sold.

You'll therefore have to weigh up how generous you can afford to be.

NOTE: Imagine yourself in your tenant's shoes for a minute so you can tell as fairly as possible, if any of the repairs you've had to make since they moved in were to fix things that happened because of their deliberate or negligent behaviour—or if everything was simply normal wear-and-tear or bad luck. How you feel about this can be a good indicator, because often the trust you extend to questionable tenants can be rewarded with their full cooperation during the sale.

If your tenants have been really good, keeping children, garden, pets and parties under control without any problems, then you could:

- Offer them first opportunity to rent the new property you may be buying (or any other property you may have vacant soon), perhaps adding a discount for their rent for the first month or two to entice them.
- Make every effort to recommend them as tenants to any buyer who may also be looking to find tenants— perhaps even including them as tenants to stay on in the current house under the terms of the sale contract, if all parties agree.
- Offer to pay them a bonus or relocation allowance if they present the place consistently well for prospective buyers.
- Give them a letter recommending them as good tenants to their future landlords elsewhere.

If they've been reasonably good to any degree, it could be worthwhile offering your tenants—past or present— the first opportunity to buy the place. They liked it enough to live there once already. They know any little problems with the place, so they won't be in for any nasty surprises. And you may be able to offer them an easy way into home ownership, where nobody else can, by offering them one of the following:

- 3% to 4% off the market price, because you won't have to pay that to a real estate agent for their commission (so long as the real estate agency who manages your tenants doesn't have some kind of preventative clause or financial penalty in the management agreement which protects them if you try to do this). And you'll still be making money, because an agent's fees are usually higher than that.
- You may also be able to offer your tenants 'vendor finance' which you can organise through your solicitor under all sorts of conditions. (In which case, you might also negotiate that the next few months' rent could be considered to be part of the deposit you need.) Ask your solicitor for more details.

An unusual solution: If your current tenants are working and willing to buy a house, but unable to afford it, investigate setting them up with tenants you have in one of your other properties, so you're selling two properties at

---

Did you know?

Every $10,000 that you're in debt costs you about $2.20 in interest every day including weekends and public holidays. However, every ten grand in profit invested in blue or green chip shares on the stockmarket, can be making you the same sort of money in fully franked dividends alone (imputation credits on share dividends). So every day that a sale slides by is actually costing you a combination of the two. Use this simple rule of thumb to work out for yourself how much you can afford to offer someone in exchange for a quick decision to buy.

once to two sets of tenants, but in a way that they're
buying investment houses for each other to rent to each
other (so they all get to be landlords too). They'll effectively get free rent from then on, because whatever they
pay to the other landlord, they recoup in rent on their
own property. Plus they'll get all the other benefits of
being a landlord—like getting most of their tax back
through negative gearing and tax deductions for running
a home office and car. As one way of helping them out of
the rent trap, this solution can be a catapult for everyone
involved if they're all agreeable.)

13

Using Property to Rip Free of the Debt Cycle

Whether you're a home-owner or a landlord, there's a fair chance you're going to get sick of being in debt if all you ever seem to do is get deeper.

So there's two things you can do.

1. You can do something about it. Or you can . . .
2. Work out the lowest and highest prices you could get if you sold your assets under worst and best case scenarios. Total up how much you owe on them. Subtract that from your top and lowest prices to see the range of your nett worth. And then stare at those two figures regularly to reassure yourself that you're doing okay, despite the weight of your debt.

Sometimes, you've done all you can do and still get that horrible feeling in your gut that you're drowning in debt. And if that's the case, option two will certainly help remind you that you have actually gotten somewhere (assuming valuations haven't dropped). But for every other occasion, there's nearly always something you can do to make your financial life easier.

For instance, many landlords complain to me after a

few years that they feel trapped in a cycle of deepening debt, especially when they've had valuations done on existing properties to release the natural equity achieved through capital gain so they could buy more properties. Aside from the constant nagging fear that their tenants are all about to turn toxic, they have to sleep at night with the fear that a short dive in property values (or a small hike in interest rates) could be enough to send them under.

If you're in this bind, escaping the cycle requires drastic measures. Restructuring your entire portfolio—including your own home—could be required, you should still try to work to your own goals BEFORE the bank gets an opportunity to dictate when and how much you get (for example, through repossession or last ditch debt restructuring).

The first thing you should try is switching loans, even if it's within the same bank. Keep your eye open for when lenders have special deals advertised on their new loans to attract new customers.

Then seize the opportunity to restructure your debt to 'release any equity' from your investment properties (gained by natural increase in property values or by reno-vations/extensions/improvements) in order to PAY OUT AS MUCH OF YOUR OWN HOME AS POSSIBLE. Debt on your own home is not tax deductible, so shift as much debt as you can away from your own home, by paying it off or reducing it to a smaller and more manageable loan.

Example: If you have five investment properties that all rise naturally in value over three years by $10,000 each, then the banks will encourage you to 'release that $50,000 equity' for a deposit on another property or two. What you're really doing is not only boosting the loan back up to 80% of the property value, but boosting it up to 80% of its NEW value, which is usually higher. (This obviously does

> **Handy hints for swapping loans at this stage**
> Make sure the deal has zero application fees, zero estab-
> lishment fees, a nice honeymoon rate that reverts to the
> SAME variable rate that existing customers are on (not
> a higher one). Make sure it has exit fees under $500 (for
> the next time you want to swap loans). And make sure it
> has a mortgage offset account, so you have somewhere
> to park your savings or personal income in a way that's
> keeping your interest expenses down.

increase your potential for greater capital gain by having
more properties working for you. But it also increases your
exposure and capital loss if valuations fall—and regardless
of whether you win or lose, your bank's coffers just keep
getting fatter.) Instead, consider selling and rebuying
properties (if only on paper) to pay off your own home
faster—yes, paying clawback if you can't avoid it by
planning ahead. This option is about security and lifestyle.
See also p. 224.

Handy hint: Switching loans and/or splitting up the one
big mortgage between two lenders can give you
the opportunity to borrow exactly the amount you choose
against each property. But if restructuring isn't an
option—often because you're stuck in a loan with high
exit fees, or if valuations have fallen and you can't release
the equity you need—then you could try one of these:

OPTIONS IF YOU DON'T MIND MOVING FROM YOUR CURRENT HOME, INCLUDE:

a) If you're desperate for a fast resolution, consider
   placing all properties in your portfolio—including
   your own home—on the market, using an agent who
   only charges advertising on each one if it sells. Then
   sell one or enough properties in order to pay out the

mortgage on your own home AND then (as much as possible) reduce the debt on your other investment properties so you can take them off the market. If your own home sells first, you can either move into one of your other investments, or buy again using the hints and tips from *Your Mortgage and How to Pay it off in Five Years,* but releasing equity from your investment homes in order to raise the deposit for your own home. (A radically backwards way of doing things!)

b) If you've got a little more freedom or time, then do the same thing as above, but placing only those properties that you choose up for sale. Usually your own home will have the greatest equity in it— remembering that equity is the differ- ence between what you owe, and what the property is really worth—but you may choose to sell one of the other properties first instead.

> **Handy hint**
> Take this opportunity to pay out your credit cards, store accounts and car loans too (in order of dearest interest rate first) so you're starting again— not really from scratch— but from a much stronger position with a bigger safety net of equity behind you.

OPTION IF YOU LOVE WHERE YOU LIVE
Place all other properties EXCEPT your own home on the market. Then sell only enough to get you back into a position where you feel comfortable with the lower debt and repayments.

Handy hint #1: Take the opportunity to 'release enough equity' from your investment properties under the new mortgage so that you can have a separate small loan for your own home (preferably under $50,000, or even better: no loan at all, and kept separate, so that you can't be forced to sell your own home if you get into a tight squeeze again).

Handy hint #2: Seize the opportunity in paying out loans (with the proceeds from your sale after the mortgage and all expenses have been deducted from the sale price) to also pay out all your car loans, personal loans, credit cards and store accounts, so that portion of your debts is switched to paying off a tax deductible investment property at a lower interest rate instead.

REFINANCING TO GET YOU OUT OF A HOLE

Lost your job? Can't get tenants often or fast enough each time your investment property is vacant? Or maybe interest rates and cost of living have all gone up and you're finding it harder to make ends meet. Then consider refinancing to a SMALLER loan.

Example: You buy a house worth $180,000 over 30 years at 8% interest with a deposit of $30,000 so the mortgage is $150,000 and the minimum monthly repayment is $1100.

After five years of standard repayments the loan will be down to about $142,500 (not much after five years' hard yakka, huh?). But if you're finding financial survival at that rate tougher than you thought, you could try refinancing down to a loan of $143,000 (the extra $500 should be more than enough to cover changeover costs if you chose a loan with a decent early payout fee). Of course you'll be stretching the loan term back to 30 years, but the repayment will be $50 less a month, which may be enough to help you along . . . especially if you pick a good loan while it's on special (eg. with zero application and valuation fees and an interest rate that's lower than what you're on now).

Remember to keep a close eye on what your change-over costs will be. If you're on a fixed interest loan, then don't just assume it will be too expensive for you. Ask what the breaking costs will be, because even if it's up to $2000 it could still be worth your while—or at least you'll know for sure if it's worthwhile waiting until your fixed loan reverts to variable, when much cheaper break-costs are likely to apply.

Definition Alert!

Honeymoon rate is where a lender gives you a low introductory interest rate for a year or two, in order to attract you as a customer to their bank.

Warning: Some of these loans have high exit fees so you can't afford to leave again. Some also revert to variable interest rates at the end of the fixed term which are higher than what their existing borrows have to pay, so they get their money out of you eventually anyway. So avoid switching, if the new loan doesn't comply with the advanced checklist on page 37.

Break costs = exit fees = early payout fees. For the purpose of this book, I treat all of these as meaning roughly the same thing.

USING AN INVESTMENT PROPERTY AS A STEPPING STONE TO YOUR DREAM HOME OR RETIREMENT

Use the principles from this chapter to get yourself into a strong financial position. And then stay there by either spreading your investment portfolio into the sharemarket, or by using the same principles as for buying a second property to pay off your first, so you can keep leaping ahead financially, gaining more and more equity until you achieve a reliable debt-free income to retire on at a time of your choosing.

Warning: As you get older, you may prefer or be forced to work shorter hours. And when you retire, you'll be earning less on your pension or super payouts too. But lowering your income means lowering the amount of tax you pay every year, and when you do that, you usually also have to lower the debt you have on your investment properties, because:

a) you still need to be able to afford repayments, and
b) there's no point in having massive tax deductions for loan interest if you don't pay enough tax that year to get it back.

So even if you keep your debts maximised for your entire working life, there should still come a time—under normal circumstances—when you HAVE to sell one or two properties to reduce the loans on the others so you can survive under your changed conditions. So prepare for that by not getting yourself in too deep, before you have to back out again. That means that in the last few years before you think you'll give up full-time work forever, you may prefer to 'sit on' any equity that builds naturally in your investments, instead of borrowing against it to get in deeper. (Unless of course you find an excellent bargain-buy!)

BUYING A SECOND PROPERTY TO PAY OFF YOUR FIRST

For anyone with a keen eye for value, you should consider shopping around to buy an income-earning investment property that can practically support its own loan from the tenant's rent AND increase in value enough so that every few years, you can:

a) Increase the investment loan to release the equity in that property, so that the size of the tax deductible loan is getting larger than your mortgage on your own home.
b) Get the released equity deposited as a cash lump sum into your mortgage offset account, so you can take it out and pay it off your own home mortgage, personal loan and credit cards.
c) You may also be able to increase the tenant's rent to keep up with the higher repayments.

Or you could take that one step further . . .

Mindblowing example: You see a property for sale that's worth $150,000 and you either buy it cheap at auction or bargain the price down yourself to only $120,000. Then you put down a small deposit of $100 to $1000 and try asking the bank to loan you 80% of the TRUE valuation. That's 80% of $150,000 = $120,000.

Has that clicked yet? You're asking to borrow $120,000, which is exactly how much you've paid for the property, so you don't need to release any equity from your own home to raise a deposit. The banks will try to ask you to provide a cash deposit anyway, or to release equity from your own home or add your own home to the mortgage documents anyway to satisfy their strict rules. But that's okay so long as they don't give you a loan that's got high exit fees. Because you don't have to stay with that bank or under those conditions forever. As soon as your fixed term or honeymoon period is up, you can switch lenders, removing your own home entirely from the mortgage if you wish to the point that you have exactly the loan you want over exactly the property you choose. (You just have to keep a closer eye on your loan switch-over costs.)

Take that one step further: If you bargain that property down by $50,000—which still isn't as good as my best

achievement—then you'll be buying a house for $100,000
for which you could borrow $120,000, giving you $20,000
cash left over to pay off your own home. (Much harder to
achieve in practice than it sounds, but still possible if you
go about your loans in the above roundabout way.)

Do remember that the interest on the $20,000 cash left
over won't be claimable as an expense because—technically—you're not spending it on the purchase of your
property. That shouldn't be much of a problem, however.
Debt freedom on your own home would be your first goal
in such cases—and never fear. The debt will become fully
tax deductible after you sell the first investment property
to buy two or three others. (See also Handy hint p. 205
and p. 224 of Real Questions Answered.)

**Don't be afraid to progress in small financial steps,
especially if they're safer than going whole hog for
multiple investment properties in a short space of time.**

**Using capital growth to pay off your own home may feel
like a backward step at times, but it puts you on much
safer financial ground, and remember . . .**

**The bottom dollar is only ever PART of the equation to
financial success. Security, independence and
happiness are the others.**

FOR NERVOUS NEDS AND NELLIES

Stepping stones—they're all you need if you like to play
things cautiously. You don't have to stretch your neck out
into risky financing schemes to scrape together multi-
property portfolios if you're going to lose sleep over it.
One property at a time is just fine. However many properties you own prior to retirement, you can either keep

---

Did you know?

One good friend gets the same kind of result without any income from tenants for a year or two. Her talent for renovating means that she puts in between 5% and 10% of her loan value in her free man-hours. (Or should I say woman-hours?) Of course she has to put in up to half of that again as building materials. So she progresses slower with a lot more effort and a lot more pressure on her wallet in the meantime —although she does sometimes take in tenants who don't mind living in an evolving project in exchange for cheaper rent. But she doesn't see it as a drain. She treats it as an enjoyable and profitable hobby. So once again, it's personal choice and 'the fun value' that makes this option attractive—that and the great sense of satisfaction she gets from helping her little cottages come alive again.

---

them to live off the income, or sell to deposit into your superannuation fund or stockmarket portfolio for greater liquidity (whichever is better for you at the time, depending on your circumstances and tax rules).

Don't let anyone push you into investing in one scheme or another if you feel nervous about it. Some of the biggest investment scams in history happened to people who were simply suckered into believing a few pretty graphs that promised them massive returns. So don't be afraid to just buy one, pay it off, save up for another and so on, if that's what you feel most comfortable doing.

14

Real Questions Answered

This chapter is dedicated to the hundreds of people who have stayed behind for hours after my book-signings and seminars to get personal help with their individual financial problems or unique situations. It's a really humbling experience to be involved in a situation like that, where I'm welcomed so easily into the most secret domain of teenagers, young couples, families, business people and pre-retirees alike—and to all of you I offer you my sincerest thanks.

Stop anyone in the street and most people would rather tell you their sexual preference than discuss the state of their personal finances; yet whole crowds of former strangers chat to me like an overgrown circle of close friends—and so I hope we have all become. On trains, in planes, in cinema queues or checkout lanes, we all usually get to talking as soon as someone recognises my ugly mug. And that contact is great, because the more we talk about our own personal investment experiences with our friends, family and workmates, the less likely the people we care most about are to get hurt by con artists, accident or pure negligence.

So please, if you do see something in this chapter—or

anywhere else in this book for that matter—that applies to someone else you know, please do share your book with them, so they can benefit too. And in sharing, know that you're helping to reverse a terrible trend that has previously left so many of us to learn about our finances the hard way—through personal hardship, financial loss, stress or pain.

> The stories, facts and figures in the following section are all true. Only the names have been changed—to protect the guilty.

HOW DO I STICK TO IT?

Dear Anita,

I am still studying but would really like to buy my own little flat. I've already made a few attempts at saving for a deposit but always something else seems to be more urgent. Last time I just used the money for a holiday in Europe. I'd really like to start saving again. Any advice on how I can get myself to stick to it?

Thanks, Jack R.

There's two points that spring to mind from your message, Jacko. First, the true cost of your holiday was everything you spent while away PLUS anything you didn't earn during that time, if any of your time off was without pay from your employer, which is scary because the true cost of your Euro-trip could have been twice what you thought it was. Second, to keep yourself motivated saving for a deposit, find a friend at uni—or a relative perhaps—who also wants the same thing and race each other to see who can each save $1000 the fastest. Then, when you both have a deposit, consider buying an investment house or unit EACH to rent to each other. Since your rent goes out of your pocket, only to be replaced by rent coming in from your friend, renting can be effectively free while you pay off an investment property with the help of negative gearing and other tax deductions. And you're guaranteed good tenants, because you're sitting in your tenant's investment. In future, you can use tax refunds to fund overseas holidays once you're on top of repayments.

SURVEYOR'S REPORT

Dear Anita,

Could you please advise me whether I should have a qualified surveyor's report done for tax purposes, as the company from whom I'm purchasing the property is suggesting, or just leave it up to my accountant at tax time. Also, any other advice you might have regarding purchasing my first investment property would be much appreciated.

Thanks, Simon

Hi Simon,

The surveyor's report is certainly a valid tax expense for the purchase of an investment property, but you should never pay for anything just because it may get you a fraction of its cost back in tax later on—that's what I call living by a false economy. And if you see this report only after you've purchased the property, any errors in boundaries will become YOUR responsibility to fix.

A surveyor's report is meant to reassure you BEFORE you buy that the boundaries on the new property are exactly where you have been told they are. If you are in any doubt that fences are not where they should be— particularly where odd-shaped or tiny allotments or unfenced properties are concerned—then I would very strongly suggest you get the vendor to provide this report to you BEFORE you sign the contract OR as part of the purchase conditions and price. That way, you can make it their responsibility to fix any problems before you sign any contract. If you leave it until after you own the place, you are no longer in a position to bargain a better deal for yourself.

Also, let's just say that you do pay for the surveyor's report for your own satisfaction and for the sake of an example, let's further say that you find from this report that a neighbouring fence is 25 cm inside your property line, then I would NOT provide details of this report to the person trying to sell you the place, as they have probably just conned you into paying for a report which they knew they needed, but didn't wish to pay for.

I do have heaps of tricks for buying an investment property, all of which hinge around the fact that you should never have the equity in your own home 'suckered' out of you to buy an investment property just for the sake of it. There *are* plenty of ways to raise large deposits quickly without having to resort to getting yourself deeper indebted to do it. 'Releasing equity' in your own home is a very clean-sounding way for the banks to keep you in debt to them much longer than you need to be (fattening their coffers out of your pocket).

For example, I've bought and paid off four properties in ten years and I've never needed bridging finance or equity release or second mortgages of any kind. The longest it's taken me to pay out an investment property is three years. The shortest is 22 months, and I can say from experience that it is very sweet indeed to own or sell an income-producing property that is completely debt-free.

Therefore DO NOT be suckered into thinking that investment properties must be paid off over a long time to maximise your tax benefits . . . I've always found that focusing on maximising my income is far more profitable than trying to minimise my tax. If your accountant suggests otherwise, then as a triple precaution, try to find out if your accountant is getting any brown paper bags full

of cash to help get you into a certain deal. Don't laugh.
I almost got suckered myself. Best of luck.

PRE-APPROVED HOME LOAN

Dear Anita,

*A real estate agent suggested a pre-approved home loan would be
an advantage when looking to purchase a home. We are having
difficulty in finding a bank or building society to do this. Is it
necessary? If so, how do we go about it?*

Thank you, Kerrie.

Dear Kerrie,
This is an excellent—but complicated—question, especially if you live in an area like Auckland, where your ability
to get a 'subject to finance clause' in your purchase
contract is difficult (for many reasons). Yes, a pre-approved
home loan can certainly be an advantage to you when you
go house-hunting. For instance, you'd be silly not to know
your borrowing capabilities before bidding at an auction,
as the fall of the hammer usually makes the deal uncon-
ditional. BUT it is my strongest recommendation that
ANY details of ANY pre-approval of finance should be
kept strictly to yourself and NOT provided to or shown to
the real estate agent if you can help it. The only exception
that I would normally make to giving this info to an agent
is if you wanted to go to an auction for a property which
you had already checked out thoroughly—including all
legal searches—AND if the auctioneers demanded this
information from you before they would provide you with
a bidder's card or number. But even then, I would provide
this information only whilst wearing my most suspicious
hat, because:

a) If you give the real estate agent any written evidence
    that you have finance pre-approved—even at the early
    stages of looking for a property—the evidence of

preapproval you provided can be used to lock you into the purchase of the property—yes, even if you discover there's a highway planned for your backyard or a hatchet murderer living next door.

b) If you give the real estate agent any indication that you have finance pre-approved, this information can be used by a clever salesperson to minimise your ability to bargain a better purchase price. And remember, the higher the price you pay, the higher the commission your real estate agent receives from the vendor. So it's not really in their interests to help you cut the price down by too much. (Whereas we'd like to try for tens of thousands.)

To your advantage, however, you can use the knowledge of your lending limit to know which price bracket of homes you can afford to look at. You can also use it to help you bargain more expensive properties down into your price bracket. So yes, it is possible that your real estate agent is trying to do you a favour, not just trying to lock you into a contract on a property which has faults that they may not be telling you about.

But—as you're finding—banks, building societies and credit unions have good reason to be cautious of giving you pre-approval information in writing. If you get roped into buying a property that has major faults in it, and they get roped into lending you the money for it, then they're likely to end up in just as big a mess as you will be if you default on the loan.

What the banks and other lenders ARE likely to tell you is how much they would *theoretically* lend to you, based on your current income and other debts. This is all the information you usually need at this stage. Anything more— particularly in writing—can be dangerous for both you AND the banks, as I've just explained. But if a lender tells you that they're not prepared to lend you money at all, then maybe you shouldn't be house-hunting at all yet until you've got a bigger deposit and better savings and/or a better credit rating worked up. (See also chapter 5, The Loan Application in *Your Mortgage* if you want hints on how to prepare your finances for fast loan approval.)

BUILDING NIGHTMARE

Dear Anita,

My experience in buying a brand new townhouse in suburban Wellington from a well-known builder has turned into such a nightmare! You'd think that buying through a big-name company would have kept me safe, but it definitely hasn't. My townhouse has been called the house from hell on national television. So I would be very interested in your opinion of the standards and ethics in this largely disreputable industry.

Thanks, Rick

Hi Rick,

I actually get quite a bit of feedback that's full of emotion like this, and it's sad because yes, many people hope that dealing with a seemingly reputable builder will mean plain sailing. But too often lately, builders with shark-like tendencies have been spending big bucks on advertising to make it look like they're big and reputable to help them stay around for a while. But being big and being able to advertise a lot does NOT go hand in hand with being reputable. Also, the building industry is rife with its own unique problems. Even the reputable builders don't actually build the properties themselves; they're more like managers of the project who subcontract each task to relevant local tradesmen, handling the money and organising everyone's diaries so in theory, the project goes up quickly and efficiently.

Each project is therefore only as good as the people who work on it. And tradesmen gangs rarely stay with the same builder for very long, which just makes an already difficult network of communication between the trades close to impossible to thoroughly manage—especially when some of the trades don't like working or talking with the others. (It's a wonder all building foremen aren't bald from pulling their hair out!)

There are nearly always 'little things' that go wrong. Walls in the wrong place. Plumbing that doesn't line up with your loo. Windows where doors should be and doors where walls should be. I've even seen a pair of giant stained-glass doors installed upside down! The only way I've found to combat this is to deal ONLY with builders who allow you access to the site at least once a week (at the end of each day is preferable) DURING construction. Only then can you pick up any problems before they become disasters. You don't have to have any experience at all in building to do this.

You usually only need a copy of your plans and a walk around the slab regularly. You'll see by the chalk-marks where they've marked where future windows, doors and walls will go. The same goes with the frame-up stage. If you're in any doubt at all *ask* the site foreman and if he can't or won't help, then go to his area manager. (The good builders will always be happy to help you.) Remember that any problems at handover mean lengthy delays for everyone—for them in getting the last payment and for you in moving in while things are fixed. And that can cost you heaps in extra rent wherever you're staying now (or in lost income for the financial year if you planned on renting it out to someone else).

Yes, there are workplace health and safety issues to be wary of in allowing even the owners access to a building site during construction, but there are also ways around this, only one of which is by making an appointment and being supervised if necessary. Do NOT let a builder hide behind this to deny you access to YOUR major investment. Make this one of the first questions in choosing your builder and AVOID builders who deny you access to check on how things are going. Your building foreman works for YOU. He should be willing to answer any questions you need to know along the way.

It may be too late this time for you Rick, but I applaud your stance in trying to make as many people as possible aware of your problems.

I still hope this helps.

OBTAINING PROPERTY VIA REAL ESTATE INVESTOR NETWORKS

Dear Anita,

As I am a novice at purchasing real estate, I'm considering investing in property through a club of investment networkers. They accumulate a number of potential purchasers and bulk-buy off a plan to supposedly reduce the purchase price. The purchased units are then let through one agency and this is supposed to guarantee tenancy. Do you know of any problems with this type of scheme?

Regards, Marty

Hi Marty!

Yes, I am familiar with real estate investment networks and investment clubs. I keep quite a close eye on these, mainly because they got my mailing address once and I haven't been able to shake their repetitive newsletters ever since. It certainly is true that schemes like this have helped many investors gain the necessary confidence to launch into their first and often subsequent investment properties. But I doubt some of their credentials in making such specific financial advice—especially where some members have only been involved in the scheme for a few months before they're talking to others about it.

Also, I'm not convinced that they are doing anything

for you that you can't do for yourself—and without any of the peer pressure, which you will certainly feel if you go to any of their meetings. All you need is a little patience, without the pressure to buy, buy, buy, and without the attempted conditioning that only 'they' can get you the best deals. Certainly look at what they have to offer if you wish, but then go shopping for yourself as well to compare. Then make your decision with all eyes open. Bargains are everywhere for everyone, you only have to look for them.

Don't be convinced that you're too busy to shop for properties or loans yourself. And don't be convinced that you should get someone else to do all the running around for you. If this is how you feel, then maybe you're not suited to investing in property to start with. Half the fun of investing in real estate is shopping around, bargaining your own deals, learning to become self-sufficient as an investor and taking responsibility for your own decisions.

It's your money . . .
Why let someone else have all the fun
when all the risk is yours?

Yes, you're investing for your future, so you'll be a little concerned about maximising your returns—especially since short-term gains by getting better bargains upfront always translate into bigger gains over the longer term too. But it's only money, Marty. It's not worth a heart attack now worrying about savings of a few thousand bucks.

You CAN get good bargains yourself. *Your Mortgage* shows how I get an average of 44% off the purchase price of every property that we've ever bought—which to my knowledge is heaps more than any investment scheme has ever achieved.

Beware of investment advisors and/or clubs/networks or advisors who try to push you into one method of financing—interest-only loans for example), or who try to steer you towards one or two lenders in particular. It's too common these days for lenders to help get investors deep into debt, and then pull the mortgage out from under them, sell them up, take everything, and leave the investor not only broke, but still in debt under the terms of their mortgage insurer (which ironically, you paid the premium for when you took out your loan).

BIG BIG BIG WARNING: Some investment advisors/ networks/clubs promote the idea of interest-only loans so you can afford repayments on multiple properties, thereby allowing you to manage a portfolio that looks much more impressive on paper, often into the millions of dollars—to which I say 'so what?' There's very little glory or comparative profit—but there is much risk—in purchasing your investments like this, especially when interest rates are low (as they are now). Whack the interest rates up an extra 3% for a year or two—which is only a fraction of what is possible based on historical trends— and down plummet your property values, your debt-to-equity ratio skyrockets, and in come the repossessors.

Ask yourself: 'So what, if some of the network members own five million dollars worth of property?' If their rental income and tax refunds are devoured by repayments and their equity belongs to the banks, then their lenders have simply suckered them into becoming unpaid fund-managers, who are also silly enough to accept all the risk.

But by all means, do join an investor network if you enjoy the social contact with like-minded people. There shouldn't be any compulsory requirement for you to buy through them in order to stay a member and their news-letters can help keep you up to date with changes in the real estate industry. But only invest through them if you can't do better yourself AND if you don't mind being dependent on other people for your investment future. If you do, realise that you're giving up flexibility and to some extent control. (In some ways, this puts investor networks for real estate in much the same basket as managed funds for stockmarket shares. In both cases, I think you can do better yourself and get better satisfaction, if you have grit and are prepared to do the leg-work required.)

I hope this helps.

EXCITING CHOICES FOR SHRINKING TAX DEDUCTIONS

Dear Anita,
If I'm paying off my investment property quickly, what can I do to ensure I still get back the most of my PAYE tax that I can?

Kelli K.

Hi Kelli,
You've got a few choices. You can do any one or combination of the following that suits your current stage and future goals. You can:

a) release up to 25% of the capital in your investment property to buy another property or two.
b) renovate or buy extra capital improvements to depreciate (as well as improve re-sale value).
c) drop your income and improve your lifestyle by dropping back to part-time work or semi-retiring. OR . . . if you're feeling really radical—and if your personal circumstances permit—you might like to try:
d) releasing the equity from an investment property to achieve debt freedom on your own home. Inland Revenue will want their 'clawback' on the building (and any contents or improvements) which achieved a

higher sale price than their depreciated values. But since the clawback is taxed at the tax rate applicable to the income tax year in which you sold the property, you can plan ahead for this too, by selling your investment property in a year when you've taken a few months off work as a holiday, retired, taken unpaid leave to have a baby or raise young children, or reduced your annual earnings in any other way (so the clawback portion isn't taxed so much in the highest tax bracket.)

There's some really exciting choices there, Kelli. So have fun!

15

A Happy Ending

Owning properties that are debt-free or self-sufficient is the sweetest feeling in the financial world . . . well, almost. Being able to sell them and keep every single cent to yourself—after sales commission—is fairly excellent too.

Just imagine it.

Thankfully, I don't have to imagine it. And I hope that after reading this book, you'll get your own taste of the same feeling in only three to five years from now.

Come on, join me! All it takes is determination and by getting this far through a book about basics, you've already shown that you have what it takes to succeed quickly—grit, determination and an open mind to learn.

LAST WORD ON BORROWING TO INVEST

We all know that borrowing to invest is just using other people's money to increase your own wealth. It has a long tradition and while some have made it work, many have done only tolerably well, while still others have failed spectacularly.

Everyone's heard about the generation of businessmen in the late 1980s who borrowed too much at the wrong time and made 'entrepreneur' into a dirty word. But with the crooks aside, many only borrowed to the absolute limits of what they were advised they could afford. So of course they became vulnerable when the tightrope was yanked from under them by rising interest rates, dropping property values and/or pressure from their investors and lenders.

But many of the same rules and warnings apply now as they did then. It's just that investor memories have grown foggy and I've seen advisors now taking advantage of that. Ten 'cushy' years of single-figure interest rates may be lulling too many of us into a false sense of security.

My golden rule for a happy ending

To give your journey into the world of investment property a happy ending, assume the property market AND the general economy is going to suffer an extended downturn for five long years, starting sometime in the next three years. (No matter how long after this book was printed.) Work out the loan limits you can afford in order to survive that kind of situation (assuming at least 10% interest rates). And then never stretch your neck out beyond that unless it's for a short-term extra-special opportunity that could generate a return of 30% or more. Otherwise, a general downturn could put you in the same need of selling at the same time as every other investor in your suburb.

In my experience, interest rates can soar to and fluctuate between 10% and 17% for up to five years at a time, so you need to have a safety net or plan of action in store for WHEN that happens—not if—especially if you're planning on having an investment loan that's going to take five to thirty years to pay out.

Take advantage of the conditions of negative gearing for now as a nice way of accelerating your returns. But don't rely on it. Governments have made radical backflips on policies of all kinds in the last decade, so never rule out changes in legislation. Plan for the worst case. And once again, don't put yourself in a position where you have to sell up all your properties at the same time as every other investor who decides to bail out after a major policy change.

Don't get greedy. Investment in property is more like investment in shares than you may wish to think. You have to try and hold onto it through its slumps and sell on its peaks. So if your capital gain doubles to the point where you can sell one property and buy two more with similar potential in another area without much of an outlay, then don't discount doing this either. Investment in property is about learning to think for yourself, learning to stick up for yourself and learning your limits—in good times and bad. And hopefully, this book has given you the confidence you need to have a fair crack at it.

SO WHERE TO FROM HERE?
Well, many of you should be rearing to apply all the hints and tips you've just learned. But pause for a tick please and take stock of just how many of the principles for borrowing and fast pay-out of investments can be applied to ordinary loans or overdrafts for other investments, like stockmarket shares or small businesses. Please consider long and hard how much extra money, maintenance, management and effort will be needed to operate an investment property instead of shares, bonds, term deposits and/or debentures etc. And then see if I can change your mind about getting into the whole mess before you have to find out the hard way that you are not suited to it.

It's only because I want to give you one last chance to avoid becoming one of those landlords who fall by the wayside if you really aren't suited to a property-oriented investment. Of course, I do thoroughly recommend

> **Didn't expect that, did you? A book about investment properties that asks you to seriously question if you should give it a miss.**

owning a string of properties outright at some stage in your life—preferably early on. It's not only a great feeling to drive down a street with a friend and say, 'Hey, did you know that's one of mine?' It's also a great sense of freedom and independence.

But you may not be suited for this kind of investment in the first place. (Or like me, you may find that your taste for property starts to wane once you've had a few.) There's just so much opportunity out there that's easier, cheaper, less stressful, less risky and MUCH less effort. For example, feel the width of this book. It's just taken me over 200 pages to explain the basics of how I make profits from property—and returns are considered good if you get between 5% and 20% returns a year (including capital gain). But it took me only one chapter—chapter 18 of *Your Money: Starting Out & Starting Over*, Australian edition—to explain how I get the same or better than that every year, with less risk, less effort and more fun using blue and green chip shares on the stockmarket. Such is the difference in the complexities between the two.

But then again, an investment property can be a great place to start if that's the direction that feels right for you at this stage. It's certainly a terrific training ground and I think everyone should have a go at some time or other at using the system to get ahead. So why not now, while the tricks and shortcuts exposed here are all still fresh in your head?

Opportunity is everywhere.

It's time to look around for yourself.

Sincerest best wishes,
Anita Bell.

Appendix I

Quiz scoring for my Sitting Duck Detector, pages 5 to 8

Question number	Answer 'A' is worth:	Answer 'B' is worth:	Answer 'C' is worth:	Comments
1	0	0	3	See next page for the Rule of 72.
2	1	3	3	Note: If you just get in their car and go you score zero for this one, for being easily led.
3	0	0	3	Always remember: Just because they say it, doesn't make it true.
4	0	2	3	Answering 'A' leaves you wide open to getting shafted from both directions.
5	0	2	3	Same comments as for Q4.
6	0	0	3	Answers A & B both maximise your debt and result in you paying tens of thousands more to the banks than you need to over the term of your loan.
7	1	0	3	Don't be a lemming and just accept whatever they offer you. Propose all contract conditions that suit you and start negotiations from there.
8	0	2	3	Answer 'A' means you're playing their game by their rules again. 'B' shows you're starting to think for yourself. 'C' shows you're ready and rearing for battle.

Add up your scores:
- A total of 24 = Congratulations. You know what you want and how to get it.
- Scores of 20 to 23 = You should do okay. You've got suspicion on your side.
- 10 to 19 = There's still hope for you yet.
- under 10 = Turn up the heat, your duck is roasting.

Appendix II

The Rule of 72 is a mathematical rule of thumb that can help you figure out in your head—roughly—how long it will take for your investment to double in value.

HOW TO DO IT:
For an investment: Divide 72 by the average inflation rate, and that's roughly how many years it will take for your investment to double in value. For instance, if inflation runs at around 3% per year every year over a long time, then a home that's worth $150,000 will be worth roughly $300,000 in 24 years. (72 ÷ 3 = 24). If the inflation rate jumps to 12%, then the house will double in value in only six years. (72 ÷ 12 = 6).

NOTE #1: Inflation rates in each suburb can be higher or lower than the national average.

NOTE #2: You can also use the Rule of 72 to see roughly how long it will take for your cash to lose half of its buying power. So if you have $1000 in your savings account now, and leave it sitting there earning jack-squat year after year when inflation is running at 12%, then in six years, that $1000 will only buy you the equivalent of what $500 will buy you now.

For an explanation of why this works, check out my website at:
www.anitabell.com

Appendix III

Table of questions to ask your real estate agent AND investment advisor before choosing to do business with their company. (See pages 6 and 152 for more details.)

Name of company Your questions should include:	Company A	Company B	Company C
1. Their contact phone number is:			
2. The person's contact name is:			
3. Why should you go with them instead of with any of their competitors?			
4. Ask to see their current proof of membership to the Real Estate Institute.			
5. How long have they worked in the industry?			
6. What was the last industry seminar they went to, and when?			
7. What property does their personal portfolio consist of?			
8. Do they have brochures about their agency and sample contracts that you can take away to read?			
9. Ask them to declare in every way, the extent to which they will profit from your involvement in their scheme / purchase or development. (Basically, ask them 'What's in it for you, aside from your commission? And how much is that?')			
10. Other questions:— (also use spare notes pages at back)			

Appendix IV

Your quick and easy annual gross income analysis

Here's a blank table to help you calculate possible income ranges from your investment property based on the range of rents per week that you may be able to charge. (See page 164, for details.) Then if tenants wish to negotiate rents within this range, you will see at a glance the effect it will have on your income for the year.

Feel welcome to change the number of weeks tenanted if you prefer to look at different samples. Just make sure your range includes calculations for good times and bad. (Full tenancy through to quite a few weeks vacant.)

When complete, add this page to your property management folder.

Annual Gross Income Analysis for the Property situated at:

Street: _____ City: _____ Post code: _____

$Rent / week	Assuming vacancy rate = zero (all 52 weeks with income)	If vacant 3 weeks in 52 (= income for 49 weeks/ year)	If vacant 6 weeks in 52 (= income for 46 weeks/ year)	If vacant 10 weeks in 52 (= income for 42 weeks/ year)	If vacant 16 weeks in 52 (= income for 36 weeks/ year)

NOTE: If you use a property manager who charges a fee that's calculated as a percentage of the rent per week, then it will be helpful for you to calculate a second table of their fees, and then a table which combines the two, so you can see at a glance how much you will get in each case, after fees are deducted.

Appendix V

Important contact details

Use this page to record info about the contacts you'll use the most:

Service	Person's Name	Phone No.	Fees	Comments
Your solicitor				
Real estate agents 1: 2:				
Mortgage Broker			NIL	
Council—rates				
Building inspector				
Lands dept				
Plumber				
Electrician				
Builder				
Garden/lawn maintenance service:				
Current tenants				

You may also need:
Banned Director Database ph 0508 266 726 or free online at:
www.companies.govt.nz/search/cad/dbssiten.main
Bond Enquiries 0800 737 666 or
www.minhousing.govt.nz
Citizens Advice Bureau (CAB): 0800 367 222,
www.cab.org.nz

Inland Revenue Department: 0800 377 774 (General tax inquiry hotline for landlords) www.ird.govt.nz
Land Information New Zealand: 0800 665 463, www.linz.govt.nz
Māori Land Information Base (MLIB): www.tpk.govt.nz/business/mlidb/default.htm
Ministry of Consumer Affairs: 04 474 2750, www.consumer-ministry.govt.nz
New Zealand Property Investor Federation: Every province has its own phone numbers, eg. Auckland is 09 379 9692 or contact by website: http://nzpif.org.nz/associations/index.shtml
Real Estate Institute of New Zealand (REINZ): 09 356 1755, www.reinz.org.nz
Real Estate New Zealand (RealENZ): 0800 732 536, www.realenz.co.nz
Residential Tenancy Act can be viewed at: www.minhousing.govt.nz/tenancy/rta.htm (or contact the Ministry of Housing, 256 Lambton, PO Box 10-729 Wellington 04 472 2753 and for a small fee it can be posted to you.)
Tenancy Advice 0800 836 262, www.minhousing.govt.nz/tenancy/index.html

Appendix VI

Summary of loans available

You might like to complete the following table as you ring around for loan details.

In 'Other Details' you might like to include comments on how they treat you over the phone, if they are courteous or leave you on hold *forever*. And make sure you ring at least one bank, one building society and one credit union, to give you a better idea of what's on offer.

*NOTE: Column 6 is for recording how much the loan will have cost by the time you make the last repayment, including all fees and interest. Column 7 is for whether or not the loan insurance offered will pay your repayments whilst you are in advance. You may also like to record any details of banks offering shareholder discounts in the 'Other details' column.

Financial institution	Phone number	Fixed interest rates	Variable interest rate	Fees & charges	Bottom line cost	See note *above Yes/No	Other details

Appendix VII

Notes pages for buying your investment property

and getting your loan

(Use any of the blank pages at the end of this book to record other phone numbers, people you contact, dates and additional information you learn. And make sure you keep your partner up to date!)

Other books by Anita Bell

Your Mortgage is for people starting out with a clean slate.

Anita and Jim purchased and paid off their first home in three years on a combined income of under $50,000 a year, when interest rates had soared to 17%. Here's all their hot tips and shortcuts so you can save decades and thousands of dollars too.

Your Money is to help you get and keep a clean slate.

Anita never realised just how much she did things differently to everyone else until after her first book was published and people wrote to her asking for more of her favourite hot tips. So this book has tricks and shortcuts (for everything except your mortgage) and has a handy financial goal guide for everyone aged 14 to 114.

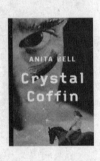

and *Crystal Coffin* is to relax with when you've earned a break

Yes, this one has elements of good money management in it too but it's a novel mainly about: *Hand grenades, horses and a desperate hostage situation* . . .
When jail is his future and death haunts every step, one 19-year-old Australian soldier must escape East Timor and crystalise hope where there is none. But can he learn to trust a girl who wears his destiny around her neck and conquer a new enemy before police, the army and air force hunt him down? *He's young. He's trained to kill. And now he's out there* . . .
(A family thriller rated M for mature readers over 13 years.)